Manage Your

Marriage

Master
the Workplace

How Mastering Relationship Skills At Home
Can Help You MASTER YOUR CAREER.

Eric & Elaine Johnson

e² publishing
G R O U P
Houston

ISBN: 0615411843
ISBN-13: 9780615411842

E Squared Publishing
3613 Goodhope
Houston, Texas 77021-6108

Acknowledgements

Elaine and I always say, "We can do more together than we can apart!" We train our children to function as a team to accomplish things around the house. This book, *Manage Your Marriage - Master the Workplace,* is a product of this philosophy.

We are grateful for our 6 amazing daughters who have stood with us through the test and trials of running a non-profit, educating them and writing a book with style and grace. For that, thank you! According to God's word you will be compensated for your patience and obedience.

Robert Kiyosaki say's, "In order to realize the success you seek; you must surround yourself with people who are smarter than you." Eric and I have done just that. We couldn't have begun this process without the guidance and expertise of Dr. Shannon Cormier and Nancy McCaslin. Your knowledge and unfailing determination are priceless.

Deavra Daughtry, thank you for your encouragement, timely wisdom and adopting us as your "First Family" at Texas Women's Empowerment Foundation meetings. Your investment into the community will reap you a greater harvest because it was when we sat (and still do) in the seats at your monthly empowerment meetings that we were activated to continue our journey as business and community leaders. We, also, thank the staff at TWEF who has been equally supportive and loving as their visionary leader.

We are thankful for meeting "The Money Lady", Marilyn Logan. Marilyn, your humor and straightforward approach to all things you put your hands to do have been nothing less than remarkable. Your out-of-the-box guidance is timely and has enriched our lives greatly.

There are those who laid a foundation for us to be in position to meet the aforementioned individuals that helped build our organization. {Eric} My mother and stepfather, Pastors Arthur and Brenda Molizone of First Open Door Deliverance Church - your loving support and fervent prayers have sustained us through our deepest valleys. My father, William Johnson, thank you for affirming me with pride and joy of being your son and calling me, "Junior". This gave me the confidence to forge ahead full steam. "Big Sis," Sonya Monique, you have been a pillar in our lives and have been there at the most critical of times. We love you for that!

{Elaine} To my sisters and only 'big' brother, cousins, nephews and nieces… in the words of the Pointer Sisters, "We are Family"! We may be small in size but we're BIG on love. This is my opportunity to say thanks and I love each of you with all my heart. We've endured sorrowful times, joyful times, quiet times and some times that I'd like to call, 'loving loudly'. Yet when it's all said and done, we're still family and we've got each other's back for sure!

To my faithful crew at St. Mary's United Methodist Church - Ms. B, Sister Mama Sonya and Rose Spencer, you have been there for the Johnson's and have shown love in so many ways that I can't name them all. Since meeting you ladies, the sisterhood has been strong. Thanks for adopting me as your 'little sister'. To Pastor Thomas L. and Sherry Walker, you, both, have supported us from the first time we met and we honor you for being an example in the community and in your home. Thank you for being a leader who recognized the leader within us.

To Joi Beasley, Phyllis Bailey and Franka Baly, what a timely connection! Thanks for seeing the vision and running with it as if it were your own. Thanks for giving us a fresh, new look. You all believed in us and didn't laugh too hard at our old efforts.

To the great men and women of faith who have been instrumental in our lives: Cleve and Cindy Sharp, you have been the leading force in our healing from past hurts and have been our accountability partners and sounding board for our endeavors. We thank God for both of you. Pastor Wilson and Elizabeth Douglas of Victorious Living Christian Center, League City, Texas - your example continues to be a standard for us in our lives and marriage. Thank you for pursuing God with everything you got. To Undrai and Bridget Fizer, we are eternally grateful for you obeying Gods voice and sharing with us what He gave you. Our union is a direct result of your zeal for people discovering their purpose! For that, we say... Thanks!

To our Lord and Savior, Jesus Christ who brought us all into right relationship with the Father, the one who is the Architect and Master Builder of our lives. We are humbled that He chose us for this time in world history to be recognized as His representatives. For that, all praise and glory belongs to our God!

Eric & Elaine

TABLE OF CONTENTS

FOREWORD

As a business entrepreneur, I find that the skills we utilize to deal with people in society can also help us in dealing with people on the job. The skills we utilize in our home and personal relationships with significant others, whether a spouse, partner, or friend, can also be used to successfully direct our relationships in other arenas.

I believe work relationships are affected by home relationships. If employees have good relationships at home, they are apt to have good relationships with their colleagues. Likewise, poor relationships at work can be a detriment to home and family relationships because they bring a level of stress and tension with them.

If a couple is happy and able to promote a peaceful home environment and spend quality time together, without work interruptions or preoccupations, their joy and happiness carries over into their job. But, poor work relationships for either spouse can cause conflict in the home and family. Long work hours and odd schedules make it challenging to maintain a healthy home relationship, because the family will not have enough time, neither quality time to spend together. The important factor is to maintain a healthy balance for work and home.

Good supportive family relationships promote a positive impact on the partner's well-being, health and performance on the job. Likewise, good supportive work relationships promote a positive impact on the family. Employers who factor in days for family events and social activities are likely to benefit from good staff morale while promoting family values and friendships. These support networks can provide emotional sustenance and alleviate workplace stress or relational challenges.

No man is an island. We exist in relationships and our humanity is based upon relationships. We live in a world of diverse relationships that help us to grow and respect others for who they are and their personal beliefs. Being able to express our spirituality is becoming more openly acceptable on the job. It encourages the opportunity for our Divine gifts and talents to shine, and it promotes a feeling of belonging and self-fulfillment; something everyone needs.

Having the freedom to share the same spiritual values with other colleagues promotes a sense of intimacy and connection. As we are spiritually transformed, our work relationships transform. We should encourage our colleagues to fully express their God-given gifts and talents, and help them find their true purpose in life. When we do this, we will no longer see them fulfilling jobs, but fulfilling purpose. They will realize their purpose is their work, and a deep sense of personal pride, creativity, loyalty, resilience, and innovation will come forth.

In this book, Managing Your Marriage, Mastering the Workplace, Eric and Elaine Johnson challenge us to take a moment to really consider what romance and jobs have in common. They passionately introduce the concept that the success of both romance and jobs is built upon the ability to have healthy interpersonal interactions.

At the end of each chapter is a list of principles that will challenge you to do better and be better in your interpersonal relationships. These principles often used in marriage and dating are called "the marriage or loving relationship." Eric and Elaine translate them into practical use on the job or in business interactions, which they call "the workplace." This book is guaranteed to help you discover yourself and will lead you to understand when romance and work is perfectly intertwine it will guarantee a successful relationship.

Grateful to be chosen,
Dr. Deavra Daughtry

INTRODUCTION

A wise man once sang, "If I can make it there, I'll make it anywhere...." Sound familiar? Okay, so the wise man wasn't a philosopher, theorist, or academician – he was actually Frank Sinatra, and the "making it" he was singing about was conquering the world-famous giant, New York City. Whether you enjoyed the big band rhythms of Old Blue Eyes (as they famously nicknamed him) or not, we've got to admit he was onto something. You see, Mr. Sinatra regarded New York as the "ultimate" mountain to conquer. Nothing else he knew of could come close to challenging him like being able to stand toe to toe with the bustling New York City, regardless of whether this included launching a career, becoming a star, finding love in the Big Apple, or achieving his notion of ultimate success. Armed with a plan, the subject of this song set out to do just that, and he was confident that it was something that could indeed be done. Then, Mr. Sinatra belts out that world famous line, "If I can make it there, I'll make it anywhere, it's up to you, New York, New Yorrrrrrrrk." While we're not exactly into conquering a big city, there are other monumental things in life that many of us seek to conquer.

1

By now, you might be thinking either one of two things. Option A, these authors really love Frank Sinatra or option B; they're making a point. Well, we must admit, the legendary Sinatra is good, but he's not at the top of our list. Instead, option B would be a more accurate assessment: these guys are trying to make a point. What's the point? The point is this: there are some mountains in life to be conquered which are so monumental that they become the standard for being able to conquer other things in life. If you can envision yourself successfully conquering the largest mountain of them all, the others will be a piece of cake. If you conquer there, you can conquer anywhere. For the purposes of this book, the monumental mountain that represents "there" would be marriage or loving relationships, and the smaller hill to climb, or the "anywhere" is your workplace.

We're not mind readers, but we're going to take a shot at what you might be thinking again. You're probably wondering, "What in the world does my marriage and my career have in common?" Good question. Take a moment to consider what a romance and a job have in common. Give up? Here's an answer: the success of both critical areas are built upon the ability to have healthy interpersonal interactions. They're both about successful relationships.

If you weren't able to connect the concepts of marriage or loving partnerships with work relationships, you are definitely not alone. Most people don't do so immediately. In fact, when you mention "relationships", most people instantly conjure up images of two people walking hand in hand down the street, exchanging loving glances with one another, hugging, kissing, caressing, giggling like school kids or even sharing a household together along with a minivan, a mortgage, two kids and a dog. However, the concept of relationship extends much further than this and in reality the principles, which govern both, are inextricably woven together.

By definition, a relationship is simply a state of connectedness between people. When you consider this, the range of what could be considered a relationship becomes much more vast and are inevitable.

It is a form of relating, finding common ground or connecting. For example, we relate in our romantic relationships, in the workplace, in the community, at places of worship, within our families, with the clerk at the local grocery store, with our child's daycare teacher, as well as the attendant at the dry cleaners. All of these examples qualify as relationships, although we engage in them at different levels. Nonetheless, they all fit the definition of relationships.

Hopefully, in reading this book, you will learn that if you are having a challenge with one of the principles that we introduce in your marriage or loving relationship, you are more than likely dealing with the same issue in the workplace. The opposite is also true: if you are experiencing a challenge in the workplace, you are most likely experiencing the same challenge in your marriage or loving relationship. Why? Because it's a relational issue that you deal with, and you are engaged in relationships both with your spouse at home and with your co-workers in the office.

Perhaps the greatest difference is that our partner in marriage or loving relationship has no problem at all telling us that we're falling short on any particular relationship principle. In the workplace, on the other hand, people tend to not tell us the truth about ourselves. Instead, they just kind of tiptoe around the issue, deal with us at arms length, overlook us, or perhaps gossip about our shortcomings around the lunch table and the water cooler. Whether in a marriage or the workplace, however, this book will present principles that will challenge us to do better and be better in all of our significant relationships.

A most life-changing revelation an individual can come to is this: the same principles often apply when managing one type of relationship to another. Why? Because relationships are about the connectedness of people, and what is essential for a successful healthy connection with a person in a romantic relationship also applies to having a successful healthy connection with a person on your softball team, in a bowling league or on the job. People are people; regardless of how you are connected to them and each of these persons require certain considerations, respect, regard, attention, concern and recognition. Whether you are relating to your child's teacher or to your significant other, you have to be able to read, respond, and relate to them appropriately in order for there to be a functional, productive interaction between you two.

The bottom line is this: learning to deal with people in one arena can also help you deal with people in another arena. Learning to successfully navigate your relationship with a significant other at home, whether a spouse, son/daughter, aunt, cousin or simply a person with whom you're in a dating relationship will ultimately help you navigate relationships at work. If you can "make it work" in forging a successful loving relationship in the home or marriage, SURELY you will be able to utilize these same skills and principles to forge a productive career that will take you farther than you ever dreamed you could go in the workplace.

Principle 1: Don't Settle for the First One You Meet

Shop Yourself Around.

UNDERSTANDING THE PRINCIPLE...

Okay, perhaps we're showing our age, but when we think about this principle, we always think about that catchy old Smokey Robinson song that says, "My mama told me... you better *shop around*." While most people know the chorus, they often skip over the other lyrics of the song that warn the young man not to be sold on the first girl he meets because he needs to find the right one that will give him the true love he deserves. Did mama know something that he didn't know? We think so.

Exactly what did mama know? Moms are usually very wise and discerning people who have gone through a thing or two over the course of their lives. We like to think mom knew when you want something badly enough, the first one which comes along, will *seem like* the one you're destined to be with forever; that is, until you come across another to compare it to. You realize that the first one was okay, but the second one has lots of value and benefits that the first one didn't offer. And then, there's another.... The lesson is the more you allow yourself to be exposed to, the more you find other selections may be equally appealing or even more so appealing than the first option.

In essence, mama was advising her son to take his time to make sure that he got the best deal before locking in the first proposal that was pitched at him. If you're like the average person, nothing is worse than being in a big rush to find something you desperately need according to a tight deadline. You want the best now; however, there's something about being in a hurry that makes you overlook the shortcomings and flaws of your current options. When you see the choices before you, if you don't turn a blind eye to them altogether, you might say, "Well, I can live with the shortcomings. Over time, I'm sure I can change that flaw." You're focused on getting what you want and you're anxious and eager to have it now; so you try to force an option to fit that would not otherwise fit if you were not under pressure.

Another cliché (yes, we're full of old sayings) says: "If you look hard enough, you'll find just what you need." This does not mean your eyes become more focused or your antennae are more sensitive to locating exactly what it is you're looking for. Nope, far from this! What the saying communicates is that when you want something desperately enough, after a while, you will make whatever you come across fit the description of what you are looking for so that you can close the deal. What you might otherwise consider to be "okay" becomes "excellent" when you're desperate because you find a way to justify readily why the option is excellent. I'm sure you're familiar with this. You say things like, "Oh, it's not *that* bad," or "Maybe I'm being too critical," or even "Well, I can't expect things to be perfect, right?" While we're not harping on the idea of holding out for – perfection – we are insisting that you hold out for who or what is right for *you*! How can you ensure that this occurs? By starting out with an understanding of what actually is right for you.

Another reason why it's good to *shop around* is because, aside from not wanting to compromise, you simply want to be sure that you get the best deal or person. You know, the best value for the resources you plan to give up; and why not? We *shop around* for the best deal when it comes to various technologies like laptops and televisions. We *shop around* for the best deal when it comes to getting cable television or a new car. We even *shop around* for the best deal when it comes to finding a daycare for our children. You see, after you have gone through the process of determining what you want and need, you will find that different people offer it for differing costs. There are lots of businesses and individuals out there who are competing for your resources and attention, be it for a consumer product, for a job, or for a partner relationship. Once you decide on what you need and what you're willing to settle with, you now have negotiating power. You are empowered to *shop around*!

Let's look at all of this in light of an example. Let's imagine. You may determine that you want to take your family to Florida on Labor Day weekend. What you must have is a 4-day, 3-night family vacation package in Orlando on the first weekend in September for no more than $400 per person. What you'd like to have is a five-star hotel, an early morning flight, a non-stop itinerary, and free tickets to at least two tourist attractions. What you end up with are vacation packages with options that both meet your must-haves and only slightly compromise a couple of your like-to-have preferences, such as, the 4-day, 3-night family vacation package in Orlando on the first weekend in September for $388 per person in a three-star hotel and with a flight that has a 1-hour layover in New Orleans. Now that you know these packages are out there, you can *shop around*! You can shop the various travel websites; you can call the airlines directly; you can try to name your own price online; or you can call a travel agent to let them know what you're looking for and even to ask them to beat the price of the other competitors out there. Remember: you're shopping around!

TAKING THE PRINCIPLE TO THE
MARRIAGE/RELATIONSHIP...

When you begin to seek out a potential partner, no one knows what is right for you more than you. If you are a healthy, well-adjusted individual, you should have a vision for your life. This vision is simply what it sounds like – it's where you *see* your life going in the distant future. Having a vision is important, because it will help to lead you and guide you as you pursue vision and attract a potential partner. It is the law of attraction at work. A potential partner is the by-product of your pursuit of vision. Vision will set the parameters for the standards that you outline for this potential partner, for these standards will help *eliminate* what is merely a "good" fit for you and *illuminate* what will be the "best" fit for you.

For example (Eric here!), just around the time that I was beginning to understand vision, there was an old girlfriend who came back into my life. I will call her Letecia. I was working in a public school coaching kids who were at risk of falling behind or who had already fallen behind in their studies. I absolutely loved working with these kids, and I knew without a shadow of a doubt that kids from the community were going to be a part of my life for the rest of my life. Letecia was great for me, so I thought. She was a year older than me, a little thin and a little taller than me, but we went to the same church and had some of the same views and values. Letecia was smart and she was an accounting major in college, which would go hand in hand with my business aspirations. However, on the other hand, Letecia barely wanted kids of her own. She was from a large family, so she didn't want a large family of her own. Also, when Letecia visited me at the school one day, something happened to expedite the inevitable: she interacted with the children I loved in a condescending, unacceptable manner that *really* helped me to see, once and for all, that she was not the one for me. This made what I had to do easy: I broke the relationship off to allow her to be found by the man who best fit her vision.

Then, there was Diana. Diana loved children and couldn't wait to have bunches of them. Diana worked in a daycare and owning a daycare was one of my business aspirations. She was very attractive and pleasing to the eye – a "brick house" in my young 19 year-old eyes! In retrospect, the problem with Diana was that her body couldn't carry babies and has since suffered numerous miscarriages. Unknown to me, the creator wanted several children from my loins, and this young lady was not the best fit for it. Though she had many other attributes that I, at the time, thought were wonderful – Diana was the best fit for someone else.

After that, along came Becky. Becky was involved with another hobby-type business that I liked. I had been cutting hair at home, a young entrepreneur, for six years by the time I met Becky. Becky was a beautician who aspired to have her own beauty and barbershop just like ME! Just like Diana, she was stacked or in the eyes of a man, she was *fine*. She looked like the women I grew up with in my family. Becky was five years older than me and was the single mom of two beautiful little girls, ages two and five years old. Becky, on the other hand, scoffed at the work I was involved in and mocked the relationship that I had with the founder of the organization I was working for. Becky also made it clear that she would only have one more child if she ever remarried. This disqualified me from the running for Mr. Knight in Shining Armor. Though Becky and I shared similar goals and vision, I was not the best fit for her life nor she the best fit for mine. I had to let her go.

As I moved through life holding tight to my vision and values, along came Elaine – the *total* package. She was all of that and then some! Those who had gone before her were not bad people. In fact, they were all good – just good for someone else. Elaine was simply the best fit for the standards and the vision revealed for my life, and she has turned out to be a dream come true!

Thus, it is important from the very beginning to become aware of your vision by creating a list of standards for your life. These standards can fall into two categories: preferred qualities and must-have qualities. It must also include who you were born to be and what you are purposed to affect or bring change to. Make a list!

When it comes to getting involved in a relationship, shopping around can save you a lot of time and heartache. But what does shopping around really mean? For all practical purposes, shopping around means: taking a step back and evaluating all of your options, evaluating all that the world has to offer. Even when you see what looks like a good deal, you don't latch onto it immediately – you walk away from it, ponder it, try to weigh the pros and cons, and take your time in deciding to commit to it. Give yourself some space to think clearly and soundly. When we get overly engaged emotionally, all common sense tends to fly out of the window. Taking time to step back allows you time to let the emotional flood subside. It's always best not to get too excited after the initial introduction because this can lead people to become over committed to the potential relationship prematurely, and once your mind starts rolling in that direction, it is hard to stop it.

Think about it. We've all had the friend, whether male or female, who tells us that they met the man or woman of their dreams – today! How they could possibly determine this in one day is beyond understanding, but they are excited nonetheless. The same day they meet the person, they begin to project into the future: a big wedding (that you are invited to – in fact, they ask the question: *will you be one of the members of the wedding party? I think our colors are going to be crimson and gold!*), a big family, a car and an SUV, a big house in the suburbs (*a two-story gray brick house in a cul-de-sac only with the master downstairs because of the security concern of our unborn children*), walks through the park holding hands, family vacations, going to married couples outings at church (*maybe we'll end up leading this ministry ourselves!*), dinner parties with their friends… they're on a roll! No matter what you say to your friend to slow him/her down, nothing seems to work. The whole "take your time" and *"shop around"* tips are out the window because they are now flooded with emotion – very *pleasurable* emotion!

What ends up happening is they eventually attach so much pleasure to this fantasy new life they are planning with this virtual stranger they just cast off all caution, care, and reluctance and go for it! When they interact with the individual, it is no longer on the basis of the here and now, getting to know one another, listening intently and determining if this is something that can work. No, now it's all about how quickly they can "fall" in love, close the deal, and begin living the now fully developed fantasy that they have concocted in their minds. "Will we look flaky if we get engaged after three months?" "Other people don't understand that when you're in love, you don't have to take your time. Let's do it now!" Unfortunately, statistics defy this, showing that these types of rushed relationships – the ones where people make hasty, emotional decisions rather than rational, logical ones – are doomed for failure within the first 1-2 years. It pays to *shop around*, regardless of whether you are dealing with a romantic relationship or a career one. Not committing yourself prematurely is important because when you are emotionally invested early, if you get rejected while you are trying to weigh things out as a romantic relationship or employment partners, the loss will not impact you so adversely.

With regards to a relationship, shopping around also allows you to be yourself without pretense. You are not desperate to make a connection, so you are not trying too hard or overdoing it when you come into contact with a potential partner. On the contrary, when you are engaged emotionally with a job offer or a romantic partner prematurely (like before you ever even develop an actual relationship), you are susceptible to go for anything. In the process of being so prematurely engaged, you can end up compromising beliefs or standards that meant a lot to you before.

For an initial relationship, connection as a friend is always best. What you will find is that a friendship without emotional attachment allows the discovery of the other person without any expectation based on performance. This type of connection can mature beyond a friendship and is so liberating! Being able to befriend someone without constantly asking, "Is this the one?" offers a level of comfort, ease and even a sense of peace that many people never experience. All facades are gone; no one is trying to impress; defenses and pretenses are down; and you actually get to see the person behind the mask that we all wear to the public – which, oftentimes is a way of protecting ourselves from being vulnerable to others. Over time, if both decide to pursue something romantically from the friendship, your romance is built on a true, genuine understanding of each other, as a person, rather than the outer persona that most people fall in love with.

An important note that we'd like to leave you with is that shopping around is not the same as shopping *'yourself* around'. We *en*courage you to *shop around*. We *dis*courage shopping 'yourself around'. While the two concepts may seem similar, there is a difference. You see, shopping around means that you are aware of your standards and looking for the best fit for you. In contrast, 'shopping yourself around' means that you are *trying* to be selected by someone in order to close a deal. This is normally accompanied by a sense of not being your true, genuine self. If you are 'shopping yourself around', you will find that you will make changes, even if they are just slight, subtle changes, in the way you react and relate to others to whom you are attracted, because you are *trying* to show them that you are "the one". The changes may also spill over into the way you talk, the way you dress, and even your very lifestyle as you modify the true you in order to fit their mold. Further, this type of activity may also lead you to compromise who you are and what you believe. Beware of shopping 'yourself around'.

☘☙

Taking the Principle to the Workplace...

The same can be true for a potential job opportunity. You find what appears to be your dream job: a beautiful office building within walking distance from your home, free childcare on the premises for employees, three weeks paid vacation per year, a salary twice that of what you were asking and other perks out of this world. However, there's a catch: you must work on weekends, non-negotiable. Well, if you are a person that is strong in your faith and actively involved in local missions, one thing that may be on your must-have list is a "weekend-free" schedule. For you, working on weekends is a deal breaker – your 'standard' list said so. Thus, you should pass on this job even though it sounds like the job of a lifetime. Yes, you could take the job, convince yourself that you can get over working on weekends because of the great compensation; live it up for a while, but eventually, it's gonna catch up with you. You won't be happy. What good is it to have such a great job but to live without a sense of peace? Or as a wise man once said, "what good does it profit a man to gain the world and lose his soul?" Certain things in life are much more important than money; like having peace of mind; like living with a purpose to make a difference in people's lives rather than simply making money; like structuring your life so you have the time to invest in your children, go to their events and give them what they need to become healthy, functional and happy little human beings.

I've definitely lived my own life by this principle (Eric speaking) Let me tell you a story. As a 17-year-old young kid nearing graduation from high school, I had several opportunities available to me. At the time, I worked as a produce clerk at a Kroger grocery store. The store manager was really fond of me because of my speed and cleanliness of my area. My cleanliness lowered his risk of being sued due to slips and falls and my speed kept the area full of fresh inventory. As a result, he offered me a management position. However, I chose not to accept this position because I couldn't see myself as a 24-year-old man tying an apron around my waist for work at a grocery store. Not to disparage anyone who does this for a living, but I wanted more. My vision was greater.

During high school, my desire was to please my father who insisted that "the money" was in automotive mechanics and that I should take classes to support his vision. In light of this, I dropped my passion for basketball for a career with ball bearings and spark plugs. On my first day of class, the auto mechanics teacher took one look at me and said (with a good ol' boy southern accent), "Mr. Johnson, you're not a mechanic. You're gonna be shop foreman!" For the two years that I was in the auto mechanics program, this man took me to Future Leaders of America banquets. He also got me accepted into a GM program at a local college since I was determined to work in auto mechanics. After I got a job as apprentice, I realized that they were paid on commission – which I knew was not for me. Nope, not in the vision!

From there I went into pharmacy because I had an uncle who was a pharmacist and two aunts who were pharmacy technicians. The money was great, especially, for a young man like me. I was making more money at 19 years old than my mother who had been on her job since I was one year old. The more I learned and prepared for pharmacy school, seeing young children use one drug and need four to five other drugs to counteract the side effects of the first drug put a bad taste in my mouth. However, what caused me to change my mind, altogether, about pharmacy was when I witnessed a co-worker who was normally soft-spoken, easy going, pleasant and non-confrontational go ballistic about her vacation time that was denied. I, then, realized that what I was doing was just a job – not a career. I didn't want to trade my freedom for money because this wasn't in my vision.

That's the value of having a vision and creating a list of standards before you ever get started with the search – you know what you are looking for in advance and you determine what you can and cannot live with. You won't allow opportunity and money to easily sidetrack you and steer you off the course you have envisioned for your life. However, if you try to determine your values, desires and needs in the heat of the situation, your judgment can become cloudy leaving you susceptible to compromise. Making a list before you get out there to shop around ensures that the values of the *real you*, not the *anxious you*, are outlined on that paper. You're going to need this list when you're out there faced with so many enticing options that may represent a conflict with your values and standards; your standards list provides something tangible that you can touch and feel and look at to remind yourself what you stand for. All those possibilities out there might seem good, they're just all not good for *you*!

In the case of a job, after the initial interview, you can get so excited about the potential of working there that you don't even consider the long hours that the recruiter discussed during the interview. These long hours will mean that you will not be able to see your children off to school in the mornings because you must leave home at 6 am, or in the evenings until after 8 or 9 pm several days a week. Yet, you are so emotionally engaged and eager that, in the moment, it doesn't even matter. You now, need a clear focus of mind because you've, impulsively, attached so much pleasure in getting that job.

Again, with premature over commitment, you run the risk of potential devastation and if you don't get the job, then what? Depression? Not to mention the fact that you, now, have to deal with guilt about your willingness to sacrifice so much significant time with your children to keep the job. Always take a step back. Evaluate things for what they are. Don't over commit or begin to dream about the future prematurely because this sets you on a course for compromise. Everyone you meet, regardless of whether you will ever develop a close business relationship or not, should be treated nicely, respectfully, and with a presentation of your best self – your best *true* self – just in case things do advance to the next level of business partnership or promotion. They may not end up being your partner or employer, but you may need to reach out to them in the future... and you can never have too many friends.

Everyone that you connect with is just that: a connection. For work, if it doesn't turn into a boss, manager, or co-worker, it's a potential network connection. The people that you work with need to like you. Learn to see value in every man and every woman you meet without working an angle and without the goal of leaving the relationship with something. If they can't directly help you advance your career, they still have value. Most importantly, you may be able to help them.

Perhaps the most important lesson to learn with this shopping around principle is this: when you know yourself and what you stand for intimately, fully and completely, this will create a sense of security and confidence in your *inner self* that will extend to your outer self and that will attract others into your life who are drawn to the values you stand for! You don't have to try so hard to force these connections to happen – they begin to happen all by themselves!

You see, knowing who you are has everything to do with knowing you, loving you, knowing your mission (your reason for being), knowing your vision (what you see for your life), knowing your core values, what type of life you desire to lead, and the foundational principles upon which you stand; each of these aspects of your being are essential for creating your own sense of identity. What's more, those who identify with who you are will want to be in your space — and they will want you to be in theirs.

Have patience, take your time, *shop around*, and you'll end up with the best!

Principle 1 Power Points:

- Whether in a relationship or at work, your ability to *shop around* and experience what different people and organizations have to offer, without getting overly attached at the first introduction, is important!

- The qualities on the standard list cannot be compromised. The standards cannot be relaxed in this column because they do not create a healthy context for you to operate in, be it physical, mental/emotional, or spiritual health.

- You can *shop around* now and take your time in making your selection in the beginning or you can pay the price with heartbreak, discontent, and feelings of failure later. It's up to you.

- Instead of always looking at things from a "love them or leave them" perspective when it comes to romance or a "what can you do for me?" perspective when it comes to the workplace, try something different: treat every person nicely and simply respect them as people. You may very well need them later on! Keep in mind that it's not a matter of right or wrong and good or bad, but a matter of best. What is the best fit for where you see yourself going?

- Allow your vision to lead and guide you. Eliminate a *good* fit to illuminate the *best* fit!

- Vision or the focused pursuit thereof, causes the law of attraction to be at work in your life, which attracts everything and everyone you need to manifest or to walk into your life – and trust us, ladies and gentlemen, you'll know!

Principle 2: Don't Assume You Already Know Everything

Educate Yourself!

UNDERSTANDING THE PRINCIPLE...

Think about this: when you look back over your life and the things you've been through-all of your experiences, your upbringing, what relationships were like in your family, and so on – your thinking about how life is and how life should be has been shaped in a way that is very unique to you. No one else has lived exactly the same life you have led; therefore, no one in the world thinks exactly like you. You and your thinking are products of your experiences.

However, consider this: what if the models that were placed before you concerning critical things in life – like relationships – were not the healthiest models? What if, while these models *seemed* to be functional, they were not in reality the type of models that one should follow in order to have a happy, healthy and lasting relationship? What if, during your upbringing, you missed certain key, critical aspects of what it takes to be a good life partner? Finally, what if you just outright missed some important lessons on what is acceptable and unacceptable in marriage and how to maintain a healthy relationship? Get our point?

Here's the essence of what we want you to understand: all of us have been educated in reading, writing and arithmetic, but unless we have intentionally sought out professional coaching or counseling as adults, none of us have been educated in how to have successful loving or marital relationships. We're all acting out of what we think is best as interpreted through the filters of how we were raised and what we've been exposed to. The drawback to this is that many of us have been exposed to some terrible models of what it means to be in a relationship. Many of them are flawed models, but they're ours, and we own them nonetheless. What's more, when two people with flawed models get together and prepare to have a healthy marital relationship, you can see trouble a mile away. It's like a train wreck bound to happen sooner or later!

TAKING THE PRINCIPLE TO THE MARRIAGE/RELATIONSHIP...

When two people who have not had any formal relationship training or coaching join together, usually there are many disagreements about how the relationship will be run; the one with the most dominant personality's relationship model will win over the more passive partner's model. Is this necessarily a good thing? Not so much. While the more passive partner may go along with the relationship model of the dominant partner for a while, the passive partner, over the course of time, will inevitably build up feelings of resentment, frustration, and even anger. Sometimes, it may take years for this to happen, and other times, it may take only a matter of weeks or months. Regardless of how long it takes, be sure you have a hiding place picked out because that partner's gonna blow!

Have you ever heard stories of the couples that appeared, at least on the outside, to be happily married, and then the relationship came to a sudden end? This usually happens because one person, the more passive one, gets to the point where he/she says, "I can't live like this anymore!" They are tired of the years of yielding to their partner's flawed relationship model, their inadequate relationship skills, and their lack of willingness to go get help. What help? It is education about how to have a relationship, specifically, relationship coaching. You know, about the stuff we think we already have under control – the stuff we dismiss as completely unnecessary – until we end up in divorce court watching our partner walk away with half of our community property.

What's more, we assume that we do not need to engage in any training about relationships. We simply go on with our assumptions that having a relationship is not that difficult – after all, people have been doing it since the beginning of time, so how hard can it be, right? Well, my friend, judging from the fact that our society's divorce rate has been skyrocketing for years, the numbers show us that relationships are not as easy as they seem. Plain old common sense and intuition alone won't cut it, if you're going to make a marriage or relationship work.

Unfortunately, our society is notorious for thinking that we know so much more than we actually do when it comes to sustainable relationships. The reality is that you don't know what you don't know until you are informed about what you don't know. Then, once your ignorance (which simply means absence of knowledge) is enlightened over and over again, you realize just how *much* you don't know. There's a world of information out there that can really empower you to get what you desire to get and be what you desire to be. Instead, we, as insecure relationship players, tend to hold tight to our traditions and observations over the years and operate out of them, whether the traditions and observations were successful or not.

On the day we married, like many new couples, we thought we knew what we needed to know to get where we needed to go. Fifteen years and six daughters later, marriage has taught us one thing for sure: that we don't know Jack about Jill! This is simply to say that in marriage, we didn't exactly know what we thought we knew. In the marriage, you and your partner will face many seasons of change, and after a while, you both will come to understand that change is inevitable. We also realized early on that what we thought we knew about what to expect from each other, was way off. The experience of marriage has a way of making you cast off all of your preconceived notions and expectations thus, forcing you to deal with the reality that you really don't know anything at all!

I, Elaine, remember the wonderful point at which Eric and I first decided that we were going to be together for the rest of our lives. After we accepted the idea that we were going to be married, and announced it to the world, we began to plan the wedding of our dreams – or so we thought. We were, now, faced with the challenge of accepting that though some parts of our backgrounds were similar (both of us were raised by single mothers), other parts were different. An example of our differences during the engagement was this: as I began the invite list, I listed all of my friends, associates, and even near-enemies! In my mind, when a woman marries, she wants the world to see her in all of her beautiful glory on one of the most special days of her life. She wants all eyes to be on her as her 'knight in shining armor' carries her off into the sunset to live happily ever after.

Eric, on the other hand, was fine with only inviting a handful of people – just a few of the most meaningful, loyal and true friends to share in our most unforgettable moment. Needless to say, the fight was on! We fought about the colors. We fought about the songs. We fought about who would sing the songs. We fought until we both realized how ridiculous we were acting and that we needed help. This prompted us to seek out mentors who were willing and ready to help us see and understand the bigger picture. You see, we soon realized that the wedding is a one-day event but the marriage is a lifetime covenant; thus, the more important focus was not working things out for the wedding, but gaining valuable tools to help us sustain the relationship after the wedding.

From that moment on, we learned to place a high value on the advice and wisdom of qualified coaches and mentors. Even today, we surround our marriage and ourselves with great mentors, coaches and spiritual guides because we realize that our power of choice is to learn life's lessons in one of two ways; we can either learn from mistakes or we can learn from mentors. We choose the latter... to learn from mentors.

People, who refuse to set aside what they think they know in order to learn and adopt new information into their relationship mentalities, are most likely headed for a collision course with a frustrated partner and a divorce attorney. They will inevitably become one of the millions of people who fall into the 50-70% of Americans who are divorcees. Do you see this statistic? *Most* people do not make it in marriage. *Most!* At some point after hearing this statistic and seeing millions of people added to it every year, you would think that people would stop *assuming* they know what it takes to have a healthy, successful relationship and would become more open to examining themselves and what they really know about how to have such a relationship. It would seem like they might actually be open to relationship education.

You may be asking, "A formal education in healthy relationship building? Is that really necessary?" Good question! Now, ask *yourself* this question: if you had never learned math, what right would you have to walk into a bank and explain to the teller that her calculations on your account were wrong? Though you've seen your friends do math as they completed their homework and you've seen accountants do math as you passed by their offices at work, why would you assume that you knew how to do it just because you've seen them doing it for years? Why would you allow yourself to feel a sense of confidence and trust in your abilities to perform such calculations? Well, this is often how we approach relationships: We assume that because we've observed other people having them all of our lives, we know how to have them too, even though we've never engaged in any coaching or training for them. Oh the arrogance of mankind!

We hear you whispering out there. You're saying, "Marriage coach? People will think our marriage is in trouble if we get this kind of help." Who cares what people think? At the end of the day, you've got to decide which is more important to you: your public pride or your relationship and family. Which would you rather have: a mediocre marriage, a dynamic marriage or no marriage at all? Now mind you, when we say no marriage at all, we're not necessarily talking about divorce. There are millions of people who still are married under the law and who live under the same roof, but they have no marriage. They live two parallel lifestyles with no interaction and no communication and the only thing they have in common is an address and memories of a past when they were once happy with one another – when they once liked each other. The options are simple for most people in marriage: you can join the millions of people who are constantly engaged in learning about how to have a successful relationship; renewing their passion from year to year and actually enjoying life with their partner, or you can roll the dice with your relationship, relying on your own limited, finite experiences to determine how to handle your relationship. We have a question for you (in our Dr. Phil voice): how's that working for you so far?

We can imagine some of you saying, "Well, I read a book..." Yes, those bountiful, plentiful relationship books. Don't get us wrong, we really do believe in expanding your knowledge through books.

If we didn't, we would not have written one ourselves. However, we do not believe in stopping with the reading of several books. That's simply not going far enough to have a healthy sustainable relationship.

While we definitely recommend learning through books, we are even greater fans of live coaching sessions with a trained relationship coaching professional. Here's why. When you read a book, it is very easy to cast aside those things that are designed to seriously challenge you to change. What tends to happen is that you select some of the recommendations, make a plan to incorporate the ones that are comfortable and convenient for you into your daily life, and go about the task of altering your behaviors – that is, when you remember and when you have enough patience to do so. The real problem with this is that a book cannot back you into a corner, challenge your ridiculous arguments and justifications, and hold you accountable.

Assigning a book to yourself to read because you're having a few problems just kind of lets you off a little too easily. You see, while you're reading a book, it's very easy to engage in self-talk that says, "I'm okay here. Hmm… I could use some minor tweaking there." A coach, however, will challenge you. Further, because they meet with you periodically for check-ups, they hold you accountable to change. You can't BS your way out of changing with a good coach who can see through shallow defenses and justifications.

Even the most skilled and talented of people need a coach. Can you imagine what Andre Johnson's football game would be like if he had a book instead of a coach (yes, he does have a coach!)? How would the most accomplished and recognized player of the Texans franchise history career fare if he got so arrogant that he said, "I can't get any better. I'm at the top of my game. I don't need a coach!" We can tell you what his game would be like – severely handicapped and a shadow of his former success. Johnson had to get coaching early on in his career when he was just getting started, and he still has a coach that works with him daily today. Ronaldinho Gaucho of Brazil has a soccer coach. Tim Duncan has one of the finest basketball coaches of all time. What can all of these guys who are at the top of their game teach us? That no matter how good you are and how talented you are, there's always room for improvement – even when you're the BEST. Remember: you don't know what you don't know until someone exposes you to new information, and this new information will empower you to get even better!

What is the purpose of a coach? Simply put, the purpose of a coach is to get you to where you say you want to go by providing information about skills and techniques, motivation along the way, and accountability so that you won't stop when things get difficult. That's the role of a coach. Even if coaches have to get in your face to make you execute the drills or activities for the day, he/she does it, because they know that in the end, it's going to result in your personal growth. Your comfort is not their concern. Your development and getting you to where you hired them to take you is their only concern, and good coaches will do whatever it takes to get you there. They'll challenge your excuses; they'll tell you to stop whining; they won't let you justify or defend yourself and your inadequacies; they'll increase their demands on you each time they see you getting a little stronger; they'll push you far beyond the limits that you ever thought you could go, and in the end, they'll stand there with you at the medal post with tears of joy in their eyes because *you* got the medal. Not them. A coach is there to ensure *your* success and to see *you* win. Considering this, why wouldn't everybody want a coach?

TAKING THE PRINCIPLE TO THE WORKPLACE...

While up to this point we have been discussing romantic or marital relationships, these exact same concepts hold true in the workplace. Remember, dealing with people means dealing with people. If you are sitting down with a marriage or relationship coach and this coach is teaching you how to better relate to your partner, these skills will not only be effective with your partner, but they can also be used to help you better relate to your children, your friends, your neighbors and your co-workers. Dealing with people is dealing with people regardless of where these people may be. If you can become effective in communicating with your partner, you will also naturally develop better relationships in the workplace. Relationship coaches are not coaching the relationship; they are coaching you as a person so that you can effectively interact with another person and have a workable relationship.

When it comes to professional coaching, convincing people that such help is essential for becoming successful can be more of a challenge, and you can probably figure out why. It is because many people consider the higher education they gained, while they were in college to be all the preparation that they need to be successful in the workplace. On the contrary! While you are in college, you learn core academics in your lower division courses, and then you progress to taking upper division courses where you undertake advanced studies in your major. However, this academic preparation is where most preparation in college ends. Unless you become a part of a professional student business organization, you get almost no exposure to what you can expect once you enter the workplace. College courses teach you very little about how to work effectively with people. Even participation in student organizations is limited in what it can teach you in terms of interpersonal relationships because these interactions are not guided. You just kind of feel your way through: if you like the leaders and members of the organization and they're easy to work with, then you work well with them, but if you don't like them and they're difficult to work with, you navigate around them or avoid them all together – and when you can't take it anymore, you simply quit the organization. This is not the real world. You can't just quit when things get tough; you've got to learn to work with everyone in the workplace – yes, even unworkable people!

Surely you know someone who is unworkable, don't you? Everyone does. What do you do when you're in the workplace and there are people who just seem like they are really out for you? It's like you can't do anything right, their eyes roll when they see you coming, and they can't even stand the way you *breathe*! Something about you just brings out the worst in them. They may not even be overly aggressive towards you. They may be very passive and resistant. You ask them to e-mail you some important information that you need to work with at the moment – something that should only take about 5 minutes – and, with a sly smile, they tell you they will get to it when they can (but they anticipate it will probably be tomorrow). Or how about this person: the one who always broadcasts your inadequacies to the whole office and announces them especially loudly to your boss. This is the one who seems to be out for your job or, if you work at the same job level as they do, they want you gone. Here's another popular one: the backstabber. This one takes most of the credit for projects you complete; they criticize your work openly; they tell on every little thing you do; and they champion the campaign to get you removed from the office because, well, they just don't want you there. All of these prototypes are whom we would consider unworkable people. Unworkable, that is, to an un-coached person.

Professional coaches are highly skilled in teaching you how to work with unworkable people, and do you know what it always starts with changing? You! Just like coaches who work with romantic relationships and marriages, professional workplace coaches can teach you how to deal with people. The very first lesson that must be understood is that you can change no one but yourself. Once you realize this, you will understand how difficult it is to change yourself, and you will begin to value, even more, the skills you will develop on how to realize personal change within yourself.

Here's another thing that a professional workplace coach will teach you: unworkable people *can* be workable if you deal with them respectfully. It's all about learning what makes them tick and then doing these things. When properly coached, you can learn how to turn these unworkable people into respectable friendships, but you've got to have help in doing this. You cannot do it alone. After all, if you could have done it on your own, you would have done it already, right?

Also, don't be afraid to ask for training at work. Most mid-size and larger companies tend to build some sort of training and development into their annual budgets for their employees' continuing education costs. You see, even they realize that unless their workers are constantly learning new information, they will fall behind the rest of the businesses that are keeping up with the progress of the industry. Your employer may recommend training for you, or you might want to find your own training and its cost. Either way, make good use of the resources that are set aside for you to continue your on-the-job education.

Here's a final note about learning: whenever someone is trying to teach you something, simply listen. This may take the restraint (of a thousand men) if you are a talker because you want to break in, testify a little and voice your agreement with the points being made, etc. However, the best thing to do when someone teaches you is to sit silently at attention and listen. If you want to communicate, do so with a nodding of the head and other non-verbals. Even if you already know 90% of what is being taught, continue listening for as long as your time will allow because, inevitably, they will drop a little nugget – just 10% of the entire conversation – that you can use to help enhance your skills and change your life. All that listening to what you did know is worth learning that little nugget that you didn't know. That nugget of knowledge could be the very thing that takes you to the next level. Also, in listening to the other, you learn about his/her perspective, which can assist in working with them effectively.

The essence of this principle, if embraced, will ensure that you have a life that is rich, ever developing, always interesting, and constantly advancing. Three simple words of advice: never stop learning! Regardless of whether it's for your relationship, your job, your parenting skills, your finances, your spiritual development, or any other area of your life; always know that there is more to learn and the more you learn, the more tools and resources you can access when you're trying to do better and be better in each of these areas. This principle is applicable to every person, regardless of gender, age, educational background (even the Ph.D. is ever-learning), or economic status (the rich read books too!).

You see, you've got to understand that you can only go as far as your knowledge will take you. If you only have level 1 knowledge, you can only have level 1 outcome. No matter how strong your willpower is; how strong your discipline is; how many hours you work or how badly you want to move up to level 2 outcomes, but you won't get level 2 outcomes with level 1 knowledge. Then, one day, you decide to take a class or get a coach that teaches you level 2 skills. All of a sudden, you employ these new skills, and you are getting level 2 results. These are better results than level 1, but they are still level 2 results. You can be happy with level 2 results for only so long, but you have now learned that there are other result levels available if you learn new information. So you seek out level 3 knowledge, desiring to get higher-level results. You see a pattern here?

You simply must have new information in order to experience new outcomes. Einstein once defined insanity as: "doing the same thing over and over again and expecting different results." Does this sound like you? If you find yourself in a position of cyclical frustration in one or more areas of your life, or even if you feel like you've peaked or climaxed in your potential in any particular area, this simply means it's time to engage in some new learning. You need some next-level information or some next-level coaching, if you're going to get a breakthrough.

If you are going to be more successful in business, you will need access to information that teaches you to be more successful. Let's face it: you've, most likely, maximized where you are now. Where you are currently in life is a direct result of the level of information that you have access to. If you desire access to greater levels, you've got to enhance the content of your thinking through learning in order to get there.

Continual learning and having someone actively engaged in your life as a coach makes the difference between those who win and those who stay in place. Quitters are people who think they already know it all; as a result, they are pretty much encroach-able. If a coach does manage to involve them in an introductory coaching session, they may actually try to coach the coach! If they pick up a book written by a professional and actually read it, their overall opinion is that, "I already knew most of that, but they had a couple of good things to say." This form of self-talk often leads to stagnation: to be idle; exist in a changeless situation. We encourage know-it-alls to avoid stagnation. Don't be a know it all. Instead, be a "learn-it-all" who is characterized by humility and who acknowledges that there's still a whole lot more for you to learn in order to get where you need to go.

Principle 2 Power Points...

- When you are ready to have a meaningful relationship at home or on the job, do not *assume* that you naturally know what it takes to have successful interpersonal relationships.

- If you really value change instead of just going through the motions of learning, you'll get a coach. If you seek personal relationship coaching, you will notice improved results not only in that relationship but also in your interactions at work, and if you seek professional coaching and apply the principles and tools, you will see improved results in your interaction at home.

- Learning to be effective with people extends to people everywhere.

- Choose to learn from mentors, not mistakes.

Principle 3: Don't Judge a Book by Its Cover

Learn to Value What's On the Inside

UNDERSTANDING THE PRINCIPLE...

E ric speaking} When my wife and I first met, she thought that I was really strange. I guess when I look back, I really wasn't your typical guy. After all, it was 1994, and I was wearing beanie caps, wide leg jeans and sandals before this look was fashionable. I felt like I was stylish in my own unique way. I even ate what would be considered "weird" food to most people, like kiwi and star fruit — not your typical countertop produce! According to my wife, the only kinds of fruit they'd ever eaten most were apples, oranges, and bananas. You know, basic fruit. Needless to say, we were on two different planes when it came to a lot of things. I had my style, and she had hers. However, our mutual pursuit of vision drew us to each other then, and we have remained together for the past 15 years.

Ever hear of the popular saying that "opposites attract"? There's something to this. Sometimes, two different people with very different styles and sets of experiences can make for an interesting combination and great chemistry. There are so many varied contributions that people can make to enrich each other's lives. Each interaction presents the opportunity to learn something interesting, exciting, and new that will broaden horizons and enhance one's quality of life. Isn't this prospect simply irresistible? Indeed it is. However, it is one that can only be embraced by considering others' differences as an opportunity to expand, grow and develop your own life.

Fifteen years after we met, my wife and I have five (yes, I said five!) beautiful daughters, together, who are our pride and joy. They are the fruit of the love that Elaine and I have shared over the years, and they make every moment in our home highly entertaining and interesting, to say the least. There's never a dull moment in the Johnson household! As a family, we enjoy life, home-school associations, community events, ministry and so many other things together that add such a huge sense of comfort, fulfillment, safety, and love to our lives. Whatever we go through, good or bad, we go through together. We're a tight-knit team. However, just think of what Elaine and I would have missed out on if, fifteen years ago, Elaine had taken one look at me, shook her head at the hippie-looking guy with the funny clothes, and walked away because I wasn't like her. We would have both missed out on what has turned out to be the adventure of a lifetime!

When you come across someone who seems to be different (we use that term "seems" intentionally) from you, there are a few possible responses you can have. You can either judge them or determine they're not worth your time; you can tolerate them and allow them to exist in your space without ever connecting with them; or you can embrace them, appreciate them, and learn from them. Which option you choose to engage in is completely up to you, but we can tell you that the latter option definitely makes life a lot more fun and fulfilling. We can also tell you that more mature, secure, winning people choose the latter option over the former. Others who appear different from them do not threaten people who win in life.

The truth of the matter is that while others may seem or appear different from you, the more time you spend interacting with them, the more similar you realize you really are to one another. The late, great Martin Luther King, Jr., once said, "we fear one another because we do not know one another and we do not know one another because we are separated". How true this is! There's something about the potential of interacting with someone who is different than you that seems to bring on an instant sense of dread or even fear. Not a fear that the person is going to attack you, harm you, demand something from you or anything like that. It's more of a sense of anxiety that you will not know how to communicate with them or relate to their differences. When you think about it, none of these potential outcomes are real, and none of them can really impact you in any significant way, but this is what paranoia about differences does: it forecasts outrageous outcomes that are so far from truth and reality that they are just ridiculous!

TAKING THE PRINCIPLE TO THE
MARRIAGE/RELATIONSHIP...

We're going to take you back to another of mom's old sayings: never judge a book by its cover. When you are looking for a potential partner, don't get lured in by all the trappings on the outside. If you are a female, the man of your dreams may not be wrapped up in the tall, dark and handsome package. Your man might just come in the short and average form. If you're a guy, the woman of your dreams may not be the 5'9" model with the tiny waist, silky hair and perfect smile that graces the cover of magazines. She may be barely 5 feet, be curvy or full-figured and come across as just a very average looking person with frizzy hair. What's most important, however, is what is on the inside. The outside may be beautiful, but the inside may be a mess (we all know some of these, right?) The opposite is also true. The outside may not be what others might call the perfect package, but the inside can be so beautiful that it brings a tear to your eye.

Unfortunately, we live in a society that judges books by their covers all day long. The drawback with that is so many people have passed up so many special opportunities to connect with people who would make an ideal partner for them, simply because they did not fit the description of what ideal and "normal" is on the outside. Peer pressure can be something else! Have you ever met someone that you instantly knew didn't look the part for you, so you cast aside your facades and just had a down-to-earth, candid conversation with them, only to discover that they were a wonderful person that could make a good potential partner? However, the first thoughts might have been: My friends wouldn't think this person is attractive or my family wouldn't like this person because he/she doesn't look all that hot. As a result of this type of judgment, people pass up what could be one of the greatest relationships of their lives.

Have you ever had a really good friend who was "just a friend," but who had been relegated to this "just a friend" category because of the way he/she looked? This was (or is) one of your closest confidantes that you could trust with all of your secrets; the one who understands you most; the one that understands you like no one else ever could; but they are stuck in the friendship zone because of the way they look? Perhaps the person is too tall or too short, too overweight or too skinny, too old or too young. Perhaps their gums are too big and their head is shaped funny. Perhaps the way they dress is either outdated or their style is very original and not what you'd see in the everyday mainstream. Perhaps they have some sort of disability. Perhaps they just look like they don't have much money. The contents of the book are great, but the cover won't allow you to actually check it out of the library and take it home because you know other people will judge you for it. What a pity.

{Elaine speaking} How true this was for Eric and me! In the beginning, neither of us was physically attracted to the other because, according to my preference, Eric was too short to fit my criteria of the man of my dreams. According to Eric's preference, I was too skinny to be the woman to "bear his seed". Truth be told, I did only weigh about 97 pounds soaking wet at the time. But, can you see our judgment, here? Obviously, we overcame our external preferences and dismissed our judgments, because we're now 15 years deep into an outrageously satisfying, ever-maturing marriage relationship. Our point is that we, too, almost missed out on the magic of marriage because of what the cover of the book looked like!

When you are in the market for a relationship, simply be open. See every person who approaches you for who they are and what they have to offer on the inside. How can you do this? Simply take the time to have a conversation. Move past their outer wrapper, whether attractive, so-so, or unattractive (according to society's definitions), and strive to see what kind of person they are. If the person doesn't become a love connection or potential partner, at least he or she can be your friend. Remember, you can never have too many of those.

The most important thing is that whomever you end up with, *you* both should be happy. Happiness comes in different shades and shapes and varieties for different people. Who cares what others think about whom you're with? You are happy, and with the lives that many of us lead, being able to come home to someone who makes you happy and who has your back means a whole lot. Learning to be happy outside of what your peers think takes being secure within yourself and knowing who you are. If you can get to this point, you'll have quite a life with your partner, and together, like us, you'll write one of the greatest stories ever told. Even if you never actually pen a book, people can enjoy being helped by reading your life.

©♋

TAKING THE PRINCIPLE TO THE WORKPLACE...

People come in different packages in the workplace as well. A 360-degree sweep of any business office or retail center will reveal this to be true. Of course, there are the obvious external differences with height, weight, race, and the other standard criteria for judging others. But then there's the wardrobe selection and sense of style that plays an even bigger role in the office. Some workers are neat and conservative, some are sort of slouchy or free-spirited, and some are very middle-of-the-line mainstream types of people. We often use these differences to determine who looks like they can go to the top and who looks like they are going to soon be on their way out the door.

Even when employees in the workplace have to wear uniforms, they will use various ways to distinguish themselves and stand out among their coworkers. For example, they may accessorize their uniform with jewelry, some a little more, some a little less. They may have an unusual haircut or hair color. Some may accent their uniform with a modern belt or shoes. Some kind of way, people will express themselves by doing something to their outer appearance, even when employers try to make the workers blend in.

Outer differences are simply creative expressions of our identity, and while we all engage in these expressions, we still insist on judging one another for them. In the workplace, there are some really quality people who have a lot to offer you and your career who look like they would be the last people on earth to be of such value to you. Because you see their wacky sense of style – or even their absence of style altogether – you disregard them, and you determine that what they have to offer will never be of any value to you in any way.

Have you ever worked in the same place with someone, but it took you years to actually engage in a real, down-to-earth conversation with him or her? In this conversation, even though they appeared to be different from you, you discovered that the two of you think just alike about many things! You are even having similar challenges with your relationships, similar worldviews, and similar spiritual values. What's the first thing you often say at the end of such an exchange, "I'm glad we got a chance to talk. I didn't know you were like this!" The truth is that we rob ourselves of some very valuable friendships and allies in the workplace when we do not take the time to engage the person behind the outer wrappings. We simply assume that we already know what's there, and we treat that person accordingly: you're important, so I'll engage you or you don't look like you have anything to offer, so I have no interest in you."

Here's the thing about differences in the workplace: we can utilize them for our benefit, which can do wonders for our career. Embracing this belief has to start with embracing the fact that you do not know everything and you do not know how to do everything. This moves you to realizations that if you are going to get certain things done, you will need for someone else in the office to compensate for the things you do not know. If you only go to people just like you, you will not find anyone who does anything differently than you. In order to have this need met, you have to go to someone different! However, how can you know that person is different if you never take the time to get involved with them?

People who are different from you can add richness to your career that you never imagined possible. They can teach you about new technologies, software, keep you informed about what trends you would otherwise know nothing about, give you different perspectives that allow you to step away from how you see things and explore new angles, help you maximize social networking, provide key information about trends in the state of the industry... the possibilities are endless! Everyone you meet has something that they can add to your life to help advance your career. If you do not find this to be true, you simply have not had enough conversations with the people in your office that you feel are of no value to you.

Learn to discover and utilize the talents of others to your benefit in the workplace. Take advantage of their training, their experiences, their intellect, their networks, etc. Whatever you do, do not consider those who are newer or young to be too new or too young to have anything to offer you. Do not consider the overweight older person who eats alone, has no family, and seems to have no friends to be disposable because he/she seems to have fallen away from the rest of the world. He or she's probably has some great information for you and would be grateful that you valued them enough to ask them for their assistance! Don't judge books in the workplace by their covers, because if they had no content on their pages, they would not be there.

Above all else, when it comes to working with others in the workplace, remember that you can never have too many allies. Losers judge people, look down on them for their differences, and either tolerate them or ostracize them. You, however, are above such unacceptable behavior, so look beyond that outer person to see what's inside. Receive everyone. Respect everyone. Value everyone. These are the characteristics of winners. Regardless of what they look like, how different they are from you, or what others think about them, be bigger and more secure than others by embracing them and being kind and polite to everyone, because everyone has something of value to offer in the workplace. They will love you for it, and they will have your back, because you will be one of the few that did not judge them. One day, they'll show you how much they appreciate you.

PRINCIPLE 3: DON'T JUDGE A BOOK BY ITS COVER

Principle 3 Power Points…

- No one is quite like you. Learn to respect the differences of others!

- You have nothing to lose when you take the time to respect and relate to every human being as an individual.

- The more people you take the time to engage in conversation, the more you will realize that while they appear different on the outside, they can be like you that it's amazing! Regardless of race, creed, income level, education, height, weight, or any other attribute, they have the same relationship issues as you, the same on-the-job challenges as you, the same concerns about making enough time for the family as you, the same economic concerns (though perhaps on different levels) as you, the same health concerns as you, etc. On the surface we may be different, but on the inside, we are all simple human beings.

- We can do more together than we can apart.

- Allow yourself to give so you that you can add value to others; allow yourself to receive from others to add value to yourself. You are in my life because there's something that you need or can benefit from my life-giving expression and, in turn, there's something I need from your life-giving expression.

Principle 4: Talk TO Me, Not AT Me

Speak My Language & Learn to Communicate Effectively

UNDERSTANDING THE PRINCIPLE...

As the highest, most advanced creatures in the world, human beings possess the unique skill and ability of language. Apes, gerbils, hyenas, ants, and every other creature in the animal kingdom use gestures, behaviors, chemical cues, and movements to communicate. You and I, on the other hand, have the ability to use the sounds we make with our mouths and vocal cords, to express the emotions, ideas, thoughts, and share experiences. Isn't it amazing then, that this unique ability would be a major obstacle in both your workplace and personal relationships?

We bet you consider yourself a fairly good communicator. But, if you'd be honest and think back over your relationships and work experiences, we're sure you could come up with an instance or two...or three...where you just couldn't get your message or thoughts across. You, my verbally-challenged friend, had entered the Communication Zone: a parallel universe similar to the Twilight Zone where up is down, down is up, and no one seems to understand a single thing coming out of your mouth! We've been there a time or two ourselves and learned the hard way that what we considered to be clear, precise, and extremely effective communication, in another person's eyes and ears, could be the equivalent of me talking loud and saying nothing. This is a lesson that I, Eric, had to learn the hard way over time.

As you may have discovered about me by now, I'm a very type A, driven, passionate, and sometimes really excited kind of person with a communication style that matched my personality pound for pound. When things were not right, I was prone to fly off the handle with a full presentation of ranting and raving, all presented at a volume that would give any surround sound system a run for its money. However, over time, I realized that no matter how much I was direct and to the point, the messages that I was trying to communicate to my spouse were simply not sinking in. No matter how matter-of-fact I got, the same things kept happening over and over again. What was the deal? Did she not hear me the first twenty times I made the point? Now, don't get me wrong. My wife is not a pushover by any means, as you read earlier. The girl can definitely hold her own, but again, we're talking about understanding differences.

Then, one day, I got smart. I had to do something different in order to get my point across. Understanding that my wife and I are like night and day and that our communication styles are equally as different, I had to do something that required some work for me. I had to tone it down. I had to talk... slowly. Calmly. Rationally. It took everything in me to actually do this – I had to suppress so much inside to get it done – but it worked. The first time I tried this, the results were amazing! My wife was able to capture in ten minutes what I had been trying to communicate to her for the past ten months! This taught me that you don't have to sugarcoat your words; they just have to be well seasoned!

It was at this point that I had a "Eureka!" I realized that my wife's failure to grasp what I had said to her time and time again was not in or based upon her undiagnosed but obviously impaired hearing, her limited intellectual capacity, or her outright refusal to comply with my wishes (of course a joke, but she's gonna get me for this). Instead, I realized her failure to understand me was based upon *my inability to speak so that she could comprehend me.* Upon doing some research, I discovered that the word communication comes from the Latin word *communicare,* which means, "to make common for the purpose of sharing". In short, I realized that I (yes, it was *me!*) was the problem because I had not found the common words and techniques needed to allow my wife to share them with me.

If you want to be an effective communicator, you must adapt the practice of learning to speak the language of the people you are communicating with. And before you ask, No! I'm not talking about learning Spanish, French, and/or German. I'm talking about tailoring what you say and how you say it to the person you are talking to in order that he or she can easily understand the thought, emotion, desire, experience or message that you are trying to convey.

So what are *we* trying to say? Different people communicate differently, and no matter how much we war with the need to custom tailor our communication to the person or people that we are addressing, if we are going to be effective, we can't fight it anymore. What effective communication means to one person will not necessarily get the message across to another, and it's both of our responsibilities to fix it!

Make sure that you keep in mind that communication does not simply mean speaking. It means both speaking and listening. It's an exchange that involves both the sending and the receiving of a message until we have the same message in common. If you are speaking and the other person is, let's say, distracted and not listening, you two are not communicating. If both of you are talking at the same time, trying to out-talk one another, you are not communicating. If I send a message to you and you do not understand what I'm talking about (whether it's your ability to hear the words themselves or simply being confused about the essence of what I'm trying to get you to understand), we are not communicating. If I send a message and you say you got it, it may seem like we communicated; however, when I ask you to repeat the message, if you are off on the message I was trying to share, we still have not communicated.

Sounds complex? Well, it is – a little at least! Communication requires both intention and effort. You don't just start talking and end up a good communicator any more than you can start the journey walking in New Orleans going to Mobile, Alabama and ending up in New York. It takes planning, patience, and work, but in the end, it will get you where you were trying to go. With a little learning and a lot of practice, you can become a good communicator; and, like all of our principles, it will lead to better results in your personal relationships, in the workplace, and in every other area of your life. Good communicators in one arena are good communicators all around!

TAKING THE PRINCIPLE TO THE MARRIAGE/RELATIONSHIP...

When it comes to investigating the impact that communication has in a relationship, there are plenty of statistics that report that it is a key critical factor to being able to have a successful relationship. In fact, communication is often cited as one of the main reasons for divorce in America. This is unfortunate. Two people fall in love and are so excited about their partnership and their future that they give up their individual lives to share one together. They buy a home, join a places of worship, have children, adopt a dog, develop an investment portfolio, take family vacations, and care for one another throughout a life filled with love, sharing, and commitment – until one day they decide they can no longer share this life with one another anymore. Why? Because they simply can't talk, they can't communicate. Either one or both of them have issues that keep them from being able to share what needs to be shared and/ or hearing what needs to be heard from the other partner; and they can no longer live with this. Sound impossible? It happens every day in America to thousands of people.

Whether you are already married, engaged or you are in a serious relationship, it is extremely important that you learn to communicate. If you want your romantic relationship – or any relationship for that matter – to work, you must learn some key tools, tips, and techniques about how to effectively communicate. However, success goes beyond this. You see, many of us have actually already had the training on the tools, tips and techniques. We may have learned them at school, at church, by reading a book, by seeing them on a talk show on television, or by reviewing them in an Internet article. Many of us know what we're supposed to do, but the success is not in the *learning*, it is in the *doing*.

You understand this, right? How many times have you said you weren't going to yell, but you ended up yelling? How many times have you said you were going to listen patiently, even though the person was talking slower than any human should be allowed to talk, but yet you cut them off and started talking yourself? How many times have you said you were going to tell your partner about what needed to be done in advance, only to wait until the last minute to share the information and put them in a tight time crunch? No, the problem is not knowing what to do to communicate effectively, it's actually having the discipline and patience to live what you already know!

Let me (Elaine) tell you, Eric and I are often challenged with this topic because we find that so many partners live a divided, compartmentalized life without realizing that they really only have 'one life to live'. You don't have a work self and a home self. You don't have a morning heart and a midnight heart. No! Everything you are, you are that way anywhere, everywhere, all day long. So, why do we change and deal with people in our lives so differently? We have patience with that co-worker on the job who we can't stand or dislike, but we can be so impatient and unforgiving with our partners at home. And, we've got to let go of "intelligencia", as a dear mentor of ours calls it. That's when you're smart as a fox or full of knowledge on how to do a thing but lack the commitment, care and concern to live it out. Instead, take the information that you know and live it. Remember, you've only got one life to live!

In spite of this, for those who say you do not already know the tips and tools for effective communication; we'd like to leave you with a few tips on how to master this in the marriage. If you embrace and hold dear these principles in the marriage, you'll be a better communicator on the job, in the community, with your kids, and in every other area of life as well. While communication is a two-way exchange, these tips are presented as if you are the person who is initiating the communication.

◉◉

Tip 1: Determine the message that you desire to communicate.

Your message is not the abundance of words that you will speak during the conversation. Rather, it is the bottom line understanding that you want your partner to walk away with at the end of the conversation. For instance, you may use several examples of things that have happened recently to make clear the message that your feelings were hurt. You may just want to have a discussion about some recent purchases to make clear the message that your partner's spending is impacting you in a negative way. Whatever you do, make sure that you don't just spend time talking and expressing yourself without any end goal in mind.

The reason for establishing what you want for your partner to walk away with in advance is because in the midst of what can be such an intense conversation, the main point can easily get lost in emotionally-charged interaction. You may end up talking for hours, going back and forth about all kinds of things that never lead to any resolution. However, if you have the bottom line message before you at all times, it will reduce the tendency to wander off into other issues and arguments that should be addressed at a later time.

☙❧

Tip 2: Choose the proper time and atmosphere to communicate.

Guys, if you are going to try effectively communicating with your wife, the best time might not be while she's cooking dinner before rushing off to her gym class. Ladies, if you are going to try communicating with your guy, the best time might not be as soon as he gets off work and walks through the door. It also might not be the best time to try to communicate with him when he's watching the game and the score is tied in favor of his favorite team or while he's reading a bedtime story to the kids. Choose a time when your partner will not be distracted by what he or she could be doing if they were not having this uncomfortable exchange with you.

Choose a time when the both of you are relaxed and can focus on one another, when no one is in a rush to get to another place or when no one is on a strict time schedule. Choose a quiet, comfortable location where the two of you can unwind and have privacy. It might also be best to wait until the kids are in bed for the evening. It may seem like the conversation is so urgent that it cannot wait until then, but most of the time it can. Your patience will allow you to communicate in an atmosphere where you will get the results you are looking for.

◌∽◌

Tip 3: Calmly Speak Their Language

Every individual is different and has a different way of speaking and hearing. Thus, in order to utilize this tip, you will need to know with whom you are communicating. Are they very sensitive? Are they more aggressive? Are they more playful and fun? Do they like to hear just the facts? You will need to know these things if you are going to speak to them in a way they can readily receive. The last thing you want to do is immediately put them on the defensive by coming at them in a way that is threatening. Instead, try to speak like them; they will begin to open up and trust.

You'll also want to consider age and culture when you are communicating, especially if you are communicating with someone other than your spouse. For example, saying, "You got me twisted" to a sixteen year old is the equivalent of saying, "You really misunderstood me" to a forty-five year old. That's clear enough, right? Most people recognize the communication problems that arise as a result of the differences in age among the four to five generations that now make up our society. Each generation has distinct attitudes, behaviors, expectations, habits and motivational buttons that affect how its members communicate and how they need to be communicated with.

◌∽◌

Tip 4: Keep Trying Until You Succeed

How will you know that you are succeeding with conveying your desired message? Have the person reflect what you've been saying back to you. Sometimes, they will reflect back just what you said, and sometimes, they will be so far off, you will think you were talking to the wind instead. When this happens, however, don't get frustrated! At this point, many people will try again, but they'll say the exact same thing as before, only MUCH louder (the other person didn't lose his or her sense of hearing, they simply didn't understand what you were trying to say). Don't move to insults about the other person's inability to understand what you consider to be common sense, and by all means, don't throw up your hands and walk away.

Instead, try it again, but this time, use different words and different examples. Don't say exactly the same things you said before. Repackage them, rephrase them, and approach it from another angle. Continue doing this until your partner can clearly reflect back to you the message you wanted them to walk away with. As long as you remain sincere in your efforts to communicate effectively, you'll get there. Remember: effective communication takes work.

Now, I know what you're thinking. You're thinking that's a lot to remember just to get someone to understand what you are trying to say. It shouldn't be that hard, right? Wrong! The way we were raised, the way we are naturally wired, and our experiences all contribute to the way we communicate with and listen to one another. Your goal is to master the subtleties of these differences and become a master communicator. Learning the differences in personal communication styles and preferences will be a large step toward this end.

☯

TAKING THE PRINCIPLE TO THE WORKPLACE...

Fortunately, the communication tips that we've already presented for your marriage will also work in the workplace. Why? These tips work because they pertain not to the content of what is being said, but the audience to whom you are speaking. People are people, and these tips transcend the nature of the relationship in question. Use them, and watch your interpersonal and professional relationships grow and develop – simply because you have learned to speak your listener's language.

What we've discussed so far is all verbal behavior, but just when you thought it was over, there's even *more* to communication. Further, this part is especially important for relationships in the workplace. Research reports that up to 67% of all communication is non-verbal. What does this mean? It means that the messages that we send are communicated mostly through our mannerisms and expressions... not our words as we often think. You see, we pay SO much attention to our words, thinking that if we say the right things and watch our tones closely, we will get our message across. However, while you think you are sending one message, because of your non-verbals, you may be sending one that is completely the opposite of what is intended.

Remember Diana from my (Eric's) story earlier? Well, we had some times when things were not so great. Whenever we had an argument, when she was being facetious towards me, or when she really wanted her statement to not only stab me in the heart, but turn 45 degrees so the wound wouldn't close, she would do this *thing* with her eyebrows; an eyebrow lift. Every time she did this, it absolutely *infuriated* me! Fast-forward to my beautiful wife, Elaine. Elaine would make the same motion with her eyebrows during everyday conversation. And yes, when she would do that, it would definitely piss me off. Elaine, however, would not have any idea why I was so pissed! We later had a discussion about it after I began to see that Elaine was doing it at times where there was no miscommunication, so it wasn't with the same intent as Diana. You see, I had brought past experiences into a fresh new relationship, thereby nearly tainting the new relationship.

Here's another story. Elaine and I jokingly call this story, "Come, Let Us Sup Together", and we both remember it well, because it was our first knock-out, drag-out argument. I'll tell it for the both of us. See, I'm a generous guy – Elaine and I both are. We both love to share what we've got with others, whether its mine to share or not, it appears! Years ago, I shared Elaine's time with the leaders and staff of our small organization. The first time I invited them over for dinner without giving her fair warning to prepare a decent meal for everyone; Elaine told me to never do that again. "Okay", was my reply. I remembered that agreement for only a short while... but (in the words of Britney Spears hit song) "O*ops, I did it again*!" This time my darling wife was angry and refused to cook. When I told her they were coming, she began to pace the floor and slam doors. Asserting myself as the head of the household, I said, "Don't you raise your voice at me and slam these doors!" Before I could finish my sentence, she was walking towards me as if she was going to knock my lights out! I stood my ground on the outside, but on the inside, I prayed to God that she wouldn't hit me. She didn't that day, but her point and message came across loud and clear and I, respectfully, cancelled the group dinner plans for the evening. Keep in mind, she didn't say a whole lot, but at that moment her look, her posture, and her stance communicated a wealth of information of teaching me how to treat my wife. Such a valuable lesson we all can learn, right?

Nonverbal behaviors are those that occur beyond our awareness. We don't even realize that we are doing them most of the time; however, whenever we are involved in stressful situations, our bodies will react. Unless we are intentional about how we are looking and coming across to others, our behaviors may get away from us and communicate something that we are not intending to communicate. By nonverbal behaviors, we are referring to very obvious visible behaviors such as stance, posture, the folding of the arms, and the gesturing of the hands all the way down to the flaring of the nostrils, the rolling of the eyes, the twiddling of the thumbs, the tapping of the foot, facial expressions, and the ever-popular scowl.

Nonverbals really do matter. For example, consider this: what message would you get from a man talking to his boss who slumps his shoulders, leans his head to the side, with eyes downcast, and looks very sullen as he says, "But I really *am* happy to be working here, and I love this company"? From which would you draw the greatest message or meaning: his ÿonverbal or his words? Get my point? Especially when our actions and words conflict, people will extract their messages from your ÿonverbal every time!

Clearly, your actions speak much louder than your words, so you should pay particular attention to this area of your communication.

Your nonverbal communication speaks the loudest, is the most easily interpreted, and has the greatest impact. But, never fear. Help has arrived! Your key to conquering non-verbal communication lies in your ability to be self-aware. What is self-awareness? It's nothing more than the act or process of monitoring your emotions, thoughts, and actions with others as they are occurring and being aware of the impact you are having on the person or people with whom you are interacting. Sounds like a lot to pay attention to while having a conversation, but with a little forethought and practice, you will soon master this oh-so-important communication component, and you'll have great relationships with your co-workers.

Try this exercise on for size (try to do it near a mirror, perhaps in the restroom if possible). During a casual conversation with one of your co-workers, pay attention to your eye contact – are you staring the person down or hardly looking at them at all? What is your face communicating? Are you sneering? Are your eyes warm and encouraging, or dull and flat? When called upon to respond to the person you're talking to, does your tone exude interest, disgust, or boredom? Also, are you cutting the person off in mid-sentence or listening quietly and encouraging them to continue by nodding your head? What is your body saying to your audience? Are your arms crossed, folded in your lap, or hanging at your sides? Are you slowly inching away from them as you talk, or are you standing still and facing the person you're talking to? Lastly, what are you thinking about during the conversation? Are you focused on the discussion at hand or allowing your mind to wander aimlessly?

All of these singular behaviors and actions combine to contribute to the nonverbal presentation you show others at any time during any conversation you ever have with anyone. The more intentional you are about paying attention to these cues, the more accustomed you will become to controlling them, and eventually you'll be able to use them to your benefit. All of them – eye contact, physical posture, tone, and expressions – are powerful tools that can be used to increase the effectiveness of your communication with those whom you work with.

Another reason that our communication suffers in the workplace is because no one wants to deal with the conflicts that arise. Commonly, people view conflict as fighting and no one wants to fight at work; it's too much at stake.... Our livelihood! We've got bills to pay and it's just not worth it. After all, we have a reputation to maintain here, and we don't want to build a reputation of always being dissatisfied or being confrontational, right? If something happens with someone or something that requires confrontation, most of us will just avoid it. Instead of addressing the situation head-on, we tend to simply steer clear of those with whom we don't feel at ease communicating. However, always remember that avoidance is no healthier than communicating in an unhealthy manner.

I, Eric, once worked with a young pharmacist named Isabelle who had a reputation of not being considerate towards others. Isabelle and I actually had a decent working relationship, which was a stark contrast to the way she worked with the rest of the staff. One day, while entering prescriptions on the computer, I stepped away from my computer to verify codes for a particular drug. By the time I got back, Isabelle had exited me out of the system, looked up some information on my terminal, and left. This all happened in about 3 minutes from start to finish, and I was not happy. I felt disrespected and taken advantage of because now, all my work was lost, and I had to start from scratch! I re-entered the information and stepped away again to fill that script, and the same thing happened again! I was furious! Being someone who wasn't fond of confrontation, I seethed over the event. I wanted to say some really hurtful things to compensate for how small she made me feel.

While seething, I was affirming inwardly, "I have a problem with Isabelle!" She didn't know it, but I was strategizing my bold, once-and-for-all blast of an address toward her. A still small voice said, "Say that again." I obeyed and said it two times. "I – have – a – problem – with – Isabelle!" Upon my third time the still, small voice stopped me before I got to the words, "with Isabelle." What I was left with was the truth: I had a problem – not Isabelle. She was going on with working, never even realizing that she'd caused my heart to bleed. After analyzing the situation, I searched for a way to address this person who had no idea of what was happening.

I continued to work on the same terminal, and eventually, lo and behold, it happened again! This time I made a joke of it by saying, "So you're the gremlin who keeps exiting me out of the system causing me to start over again." She laughed with me because I was *her* gremlin who kept using that terminal! Our relationship changed that day. I learned how to cope with confrontation in a new, positive and productive way. Isabelle learned how to ask if someone was using a terminal before using it herself. From that day forward, whenever Isabelle and I worked the weekend shift together, she would buy my breakfast. Sweet deal huh? My advice to you: step back from the situation, relax and take a few breaths, give yourself a little time, and then figure out how you can communicate your message in a calm, non-threatening manner.

Finally, when it comes to the workplace, there are three tips, in addition to the ones that we presented for the marriage, which if applied, can take your communication game to the next level:

❦

Tip 1: Communicate Frequently

There's nothing like working with a person who stays in a vacuum. You know, the one who receives information, but they like to store it up until just the right time and present it to others perhaps once a week – an introvert. Wouldn't you like to know information that will affect or impact your job as soon as it is available? Well, you're not alone. Others desire the same thing.

As soon as you get information that will impact others or that they should simply know for informational purposes, communicate it; face-to-face, through e-mail, memos, text message and by phone calls as soon as information comes to your desk. Don't just inform of business topics once a day, communicate as many times as necessary. Your co-workers will appreciate you for keeping them in the loop and for communicating in such a timely manner because it will help them get their job done even better.

❦

Tip 2: Communicate with Intention

Especially when you are communicating face-to-face in the office, make certain that you are not just talking passively. Remember to have your message in mind before you ever get started. Know before you approach the other persons what you want them to walk away with, and speak to them with this goal in mind. Find a time and place to communicate with them that are comfortable and convenient for them (if you want to get the results). Speak their language with words and examples they can understand; get in their world, and if they don't get it the first time, keep trying! Also, don't forget to pay attention to your ÿonverbal and how you are coming across as you speak and listen to them, and pay attention to theirs as well. Yes, it seems like a lot, but effectiveness takes work.

ⓒⓎ

Tip 3: Communicate with As Many People as Possible!

It's always good to share whatever news, updates, or information you have with as many people as might be impacted in the office. Even the smallest tidbits of progress or updates may be of interest to others. What you don't want to be known as is "the territorial one" in the office who receives information and updates but only shares with particular people on a "need-to-know" basis. Sharing business updates and information with as many co-workers as possible will position you, in the workplace, as someone who is cooperative; a team player, willing to share, and who wants to see everyone succeed!

Although human beings are uniquely gifted with the ability to speak, the ability to communicate is not a foregone conclusion for the great majority of society. However, with a little intention and attention to details, you can improve your ability to convey anything to anyone. Once you focus on making the message you are passing on common, take into consideration your listener's age and personality, then master the non-verbal cues you send while you speak. You will be well on your way to becoming, not simply, an effective communicator, but one who has mastered the art of communicating expertly.

❦

Here's a process to follow when communication is difficult:

1. Write down what you heard communicated and *feel it through*!
    - "Feel It Through" – own and feel every emotion. Don't act on them! Just let your feelings run their course.
2. Step out of the situation – look at what was just said as an outsider looking in. Do this from a sober place, preferably after "feeling it through." Sometimes our emotions can impair our judgment.
3. Evaluate the situation
    - How you heard it
    - What was said, how it was said, and what it meant to you
    - Form questions you would like to ask your partner/coworker that can eliminate or confirm perceptions and assumptions
4. Respond soberly
5. Actively listen and hear – take what is said for face value until a pattern emerges
6. Repeat until the issue is resolved

Exercises for Maintaining Open Communication

1. 5 minutes – This is where within the first five minutes of you seeing your partner after work, you greet, embrace, and get into each other's world. If the first five minutes are not doable, make it before you prepare for bed. Not when you get in the bed, but before you even go into the bedroom.

    a.   I know we mentioned that right after work may not be the best time for this type of communication, and this position is widely held in mainstream media; however, it's a matter of behavior and it can be done. The myth that men don't like to talk is a lie. Before men marry their women, they can talk on the phone all night. Men will stay on the phone until 2 AM with their girlfriends, knowing the whole time that they must get out of bed by 6 AM to go to work. If a man can do this during courtship, he can do it to maintain his marriage. During courtship, there is relatively not much to talk about; however, after marriage, there is a lot to talk about! Kids, work, vacation, family vision/goals or even date night to name a few. If men can talk to the fellas at work, certainly they can talk to their partners at home.

    b.   This is a place where you are able to find out many details about your partner without directly asking him or her. Create a safe place for them to share their heart, and they'll give it to you. When I go through this exercise, I learn things I didn't know in this time. I get gift ideas from this time. I know what issues are going on in Elaine's world from this time. With this information, I can position myself to be the hero or simply ask for help from the divine on matters of her heart. How do you think I got my five daughters?

2.   7 minutes – This is non-sensual and non-verbal. For 5 minutes, stand up and embrace your partner. Close your eyes and feel their heart beat. Feel their chest rise and fall with every breath. After 5 minutes, look into each other's eyes for the remaining 2 minutes. For the first few times you do this you'll feel so vulnerable, but that's the point. You can stick to the time limits until you develop your own flow with it.

3.   Marital Maintenance – This is an evaluation of each other's performance in the relationship. Just as on the job you

get evaluated and receive a performance objective plan, an outline of things you will do better, and an overview of what you will continue to do well in. In a relationship, you should have similar evaluations. With this exercise, praise is openly given, and issues don't sneak up, they're brought up. A plan is developed to help you guys continue to excel and lay out a plan for areas you need to improve upon.

∞

Principle 4 Power Points...

- Communication is not a one-size-fits-all technique. You must learn how different people communicate and then custom fit your communication method to best suit each person – that is, if you want to communicate effectively.

- Rome was not built in a day. Neither will you become an expert communicator overnight. Don't set unrealistic expectations. Instead, incorporate the principles of effective communication into your conversations gradually and look for the small wins.

- Develop the discipline to walk out or live what you already know because you only have one life to live.

- Teach people how to treat you – well.

- Perfect practice makes perfect. If necessary, take five minutes a day and talk to yourself in the mirror or ask a friend to critique your non-verbal cues during a five-minute discussion. Listen to their feedback and use it as a tool for improvement.

Principle 5: Accept
Differences in Knowledge

Take "You Should Know This"
Out of Your Vocabulary!

UNDERSTANDING THE PRINCIPLE...

F unny word, "should". Even though it's not a four-letter word, it sure packs quite a punch. Don't believe it? Well, take it from someone who knows what it's like to experience the nuclear bomb that can be released as a result of the improper and causal use of this innocuous looking, and sounding, word. After all, its very connotation is one of expectation of likelihood or probability of something happening based on a particular scheduled time. Let me share a true story with you.

Growing up, I, Eric, was raised by a hard working single mother. My mother was determined to raise a son that would not have a woman waiting on him hand and foot. No, the son she raised would be self-sufficient and able to carry a household, especially ensuring that things didn't shut down in the house after babies were born, and she made sure of this by training me in every domestic household duty possible. Mom taught me to do it all: cooking, cleaning, laundry, pumping the gas – you name it, I learned it. In fact, I ended up learning more about running a household than many of the women that I came into contact with over the years. It was my mother's goal to make her son an asset to the woman that would be privileged enough to eventually marry him, and I've got to admit it – she did a great job.

Fast-forward the story to the era of inhabiting a home with my wife, Elaine. Ahhh, sweet Elaine. She's the love of my life, but I've got to admit it: I'm much better than her when it comes to domestic duties in the household. Case in point: laundry. When we first got married, I was the expert, and she... well, let's just say she wasn't.

Newly married, Elaine and I had an incident in the washroom. We like to refer to this one as the "Not-So-Clean Communication in the Washroom" situation. Today, we laugh about it, but back then, it was a serious matter! After an otherwise very ordinary washday, I had pulled a pair of my jeans out of the machine, and I was surprised to find a large clump of sticky, white washing powder on them. I hit the roof! To say the least, there was a verbal altercation between us, followed by a hastily delivered, rather excited detailed lesson on how one is supposed to wash clothes properly. Of course, looking back on the matter, I understand that I could have reacted a little differently... well, a lot differently. However, my anger was fueled by a false assumption. What was this assumption? I assumed that my wife should have known how to do laundry as well as I did.

Unfortunately, not only was this assumption something I believed, it was something I expressed freely and as passionately as possible to my slightly offended and highly surprised wife, as I stood in the laundry room holding my washing-powder clumped jeans. In response to my "should" assertion, which actually probably felt more like an accusation, my wife, who is no pushover, immediately proceeded to tell me, first of all, that she didn't appreciate my tone, and then she went into how I was the most pompous and condescending man she had ever met. At the time of the argument, I couldn't fathom the words that were coming out of my wife's mouth in rapid-fire succession. However, later that night, as I struggled to find a comfortable position on our living room sofa, I had an epiphany. My wife was 100% right. I had behaved arrogantly. Telling my wife that she "should" have known how to wash clothes properly was the equivalent of calling her stupid and inept; a fact that was not lost on her.

I must say that during this situation, after realizing that my approach was a bit insensitive, I apologized. However, Elaine's feelings were so hurt that we sought out non-biased counsel. It was then that my wife helped me understand her background. My wife was the youngest in her family and by the time she was five years old, she became an aunt, which meant that her older sisters had to mother their own babies and her single mom had the concerns of providing for her children. As a result, the focus was not so much on passing down domestic duties to the younger girls. This insight helped me to understand my wife better, and this helped us to grow together in many ways.

'Rise above your raising' was the lesson gained. When you become someone's partner in a relationship, your upbringing is now being meshed with another's. Neither partner's upbringing should be categorized as wrong or right or greater or lesser. Some principles you learned coming up might have worked for certain situations and other things you learned don't work so well. You and your partner have to come together and agree on this. However, know that neither of you will act nor think the same, because you are *not* the same! I like to use the example of mountains. Major mountain ranges are created when the earth's tectonic plates crash together. The more they oppose each other, the more the come together, go higher and become one. Thus, it's not always about how you were raised, but how you are rising.

☙❧

TAKING THE PRINCIPLE INTO THE MARRIAGE...

As a result of the true experience I just shared with you about Elaine, I began to examine and pay attention to how often I used the word "should" when speaking to or dealing with others. I was surprised by what I found. I discovered that a "should mentality" pervaded my daily, interpersonal interactions. Even more than that, I started listening to other people, and I realized that a lot of us use the word "should" with our partners in marriage and loving relationships. What was the harm in this way of thinking? Glad you asked!

When we use the word "should" on our partner, we are basically expressing an expectation. We are saying that we expect them to think a certain way or perform in a certain capacity. However, what often goes overlooked is the fact that our expectations in the marriage must have a basis or a reason for being expected. In other words, I expect this of you, but why? With Elaine, I had no such basis for my expectation. Using the word "should" also suggests that the probability of the person we're talking to being able to think or perform in this way is high, and that they *should* (there's that word again) be able to think or perform this way by now. It takes a lot of assuming on your part to come up with an expectation of another person.

Wow, that's a mouthful! In the same regard, these expectations that we impose on others can also be a mouthful. What gives us the right to have a "should" expectation of others without having full disclosure of their upbringing, background, education, temperament, conditioning, experiences, mindset, and anything else that has gone into shaping who and how they are? What's more, what gives us the right to expect these things at this particular point in time? What shapes these expectations? What allows us to put these demands on people's experiences and time? Get the point?

As you can see, I learned the hard way that this little, six-letter word has no place in personal relationships when discussing or addressing your expectations about what you believe your spouse should know or understand. Using the word "should" is tantamount to saying "I know that, so why don't *you* know? What's wrong with you that you don't know something as basic as that?" Used in this way, this word has the ability to create animosity, resentment, and eventually disrespect between you and your loved one.

In order to prevent these feelings from developing, you must learn to accept your partner's knowledge differences. This is the very first step in avoiding the use of the s-word. Research scientists have discovered that while men and women can reach similar conclusions and make similar decisions, the processes they use to do so are quite dissimilar. Women are broad thinkers who process a lot of information and base their decisions on this wide range of information. By contrast, men are more linear thinkers who rely on a progression of thoughts and ideas to reach their conclusions. Neither method of knowledge processing is superior to the other. It's simply an indication of the way we are wired. Women and men are just plain different.

What other practical steps can you take in order to avoid the destruction caused by using the s-word in your personal relationships? Glad you asked! The second step in conquering a "should"- mentality involves extending the respect you would expect from your spouse to him or her when you discover a knowledge area in which she/he is lacking and using these moments to share and build intimacy with your loved one. No one involved in a fulfilling relationship would intentionally set out to or derive pleasure from demeaning or degrading his/her significant other by insulting their intelligence. As such, commit to creating a bonding experience for you and your partner. Offer to share what you know in as gentle a manner as possible, but be prepared for his/her possible refusal. However, if your offer is accepted, share what you know in a light-hearted manner. Don't talk down to your partner. Rather, use the opportunity as a relationship building experience that can endear you to one another as one shares, and the other receives the information in question.

Another important step is to understand the bond of strengths and weaknesses. Is there such a thing? Absolutely! In successful relationships, it is realized that one person's weakness is another person's strength. There will be times when one is weak and the other must be strong and vice versa. When this is understood, individuals can continue to be themselves and grow from their place of strength and natural ability.

TAKING THE PRINCIPLE INTO THE WORKPLACE...

The existence of a you-should-know-this mentality can be just as devastating in the workplace as your home. In fact, it can be more devastating if several employees or team-members exhibit this mindset. A you-should-know-this attitude between common team-members can have excruciating effects on the team-members to whom these attitudes are directed. These attitudes can result in the ostracism, ridicule, and not-so-innocent stereotyping of a team member who has been identified or is believed to be less capable of performing and producing the same level as his or her team-mates.

However, the more likely instance is the existence of this attitude and the use of this phrase by a manager or team-lead. Consider a supervisor who exhibits this attitude toward his or her employees. How high do you think their morale would be? How productive and creative do you think they could be in an environment like that? Better yet, how long do you think they would tolerate being talked down to and being subjected to such self-esteem lowering comments? We're willing to bet that the manager's team would be one of the lowest-producing teams in the organization, and it would likely have one of the highest turnover rates too.

The act of addressing "should" attitudes in the workplace is done more easily in a professional setting than at home. In most organizations, employees' developmental needs are evaluated and addressed at regularly scheduled intervals. These evaluations are aimed at increasing employees' abilities to perform via training and by increasing job responsibilities. However, there are several practical steps you can take individually in order to improve the relationships you have with your co-workers or employees.

In order to eradicate this attitude in your thinking, be willing to extend grace to others when it's discovered that an employee is lacking knowledge in a particular area or related to specific subject matter. A good manager or team member always finds ways to improve his/her fellow employees. Recognize deficiencies in your colleagues' knowledge and expertise and train yourself to see them as personal teaching and training opportunities. Become a humble champion for their improvement, and watch the creativity, self-esteem and productivity of your group or co-workers soar!

Principle 5 Power Points...

- The more you learn, the more you realize how much more there is you need to learn! Just because you have had the privilege of learning something along your journey, never assume that others have learned the same lessons on their own journey – and never disparage them for it. The best way to do this is to remove the word "should" from your vocabulary.

- The more we examine why we feel we have the right to expect people to think, respond, or perform a certain way, the more we begin to understand how irrational the use of "should" really is in most situations.

- Make a "should" list. Note how many times you use it in a day and practice removing it from your vocabulary.

Principle 6: Have a Heart for People

A Little Empathy Goes a Long Way in Successful Relationships

UNDERSTANDING THE PRINCIPLE...

Way back in 1980, economist John Naisbitt wrote the New York Times bestseller book *Megatrends*. In the book, Naisbitt described the major patterns and trends that would affect America and the world in the future. One of the most significant trends he predicted was that the world would become increasingly consumed and driven by electronics and technology and less involved with interpersonal relationships and face-to-face human interactions. Naisbitt called this trend "high-tech, low touch" and claimed it would affect the very fabric of American culture. Although the increase in technology would put the world at our fingertips, unless compensated for and addressed, the technology sub trend future would also change the way people meet and date, families interact and would highly impact the amount of time we spent interacting and communicating with other human beings.

Did this writer know what he was talking about or did he miss the boat on his techno-theory? Well, let's step back and look around. Once only the stuff of science-fiction movies; Blackberries,

Palm Pilots, GPS, and other electronic gadgets are now commonplace for not only adults but also teenagers and children around the world. Computers, which were once very expensive and found only in the homes of the very rich, are now found, two and three at a time in varying sizes and capacities, in more homes than not from coast to coast. Millions of people use social networking sites such as MySpace and Facebook on a daily basis to "talk" to their friends and family. Web-conferences, webinars and online meetings are increasingly being used to replace face-to-face meetings and gatherings. Naisbitt's techno-theory became manifest.

Directly related to the "high-tech, low-touch" phenomenon is a trend recently identified and labeled by the American Psychiatric Association as Empathy Deficit Disorder (EDD). EDD? Wow... who knew that there could even be such a thing? This brings us to the question: What is empathy and why is it important to me?

By and large, the way we behave, communicate, and allow ourselves to feel and express emotions is the result of the way we were raised. So, as a child, you either learned that it was okay to express and share your feelings or that it was not okay. You either learned to be sensitive to the needs of others or you were taught to look out for yourself. Case in point: (Elaine speaking) As a teenager, when my siblings and I found ourselves disappointed by one of our friends or questioned the motives behind someone's actions, our mother would look at us sternly and warn us not to judge or criticize someone else until we had "walked a mile in his shoes." In essence, mom was simply trying to teach us to be empathetic.

Right about here, people start asking themselves "What is the difference between empathy and sympathy?" Merriam-Webster defines *sympathy* as "the act or capacity of entering into or sharing the feelings or interests of another and the emotional and mental state that results due to the sensitivity experienced." In short, sympathy is the act of feeling emotions, usually of unhappiness or sadness, as a result of another person's experience.

On the other hand, *empathy* is defined as "the action of understanding, being aware of, being sensitive to, and vicariously experiencing the feelings, thoughts, and experience of another of either the past or present without having the feelings, thoughts, and experience communicated to them." A person who feels empathy for someone else can understand and even reflect another person's thoughts and emotions.

Although we may not have had the exact same experiences as another person, empathy allows us to make emotional connections with other people. A wise man once said, "empathy is to see with the eyes of another; to hear with the ears of another; and to feel with the heart of another." When you empathize with someone, their world becomes yours and you experience their emotions, feelings, and frustrations. Unfortunately, many Americans have lost, or were never taught the all important emotional/relational tool of empathy which has created the EDD – Empathy Deficient Disorder – crisis we are now experiencing. In short, we live in a society that simply doesn't care about the issues, problems, and concerns of others around us. We have become an empathy-deficient people.

How do *Megatrends,* a high-tech, low-touch society and empathy all tie in together? Most of us are not immune to experiencing EDD. If you were born during the last 40 years, very likely, you are deficient in the way you empathize with others. Unfortunately, this deficiency can have devastating effects on both your personal and professional relationships.

Let's see. By now we're sure you're having one of two reactions. You're either shaking your head or thinking "No, that's not me. I know I empathize with others," or you're not quite sure. Well to put your mind at ease, consider how you would respond to the following two scenarios:

First: It's Thursday evening, and you're just getting home from work. Dinner needs to be cooked and the kids need to be attended to, neither of which is your regular duty. What do you do? If your response is something along the lines of pitching in to help out in order to prevent your significant other from ranting and raving for the rest of the evening, you likely have a bit of an empathy problem.

Second: During a casual evening together, the person you are dating opens up and begins sharing some details with you about their previous dating relationships. Do you listen and participate in the conversation because you know it's the right thing to do; you don't want to hurt their feelings, or because you know what it's like to need to talk. If your motivation for doing or not doing something is based upon trying to avoid an argument with your partner, then you're not being empathetic.

Remember, the key to being empathetic is having the ability to "walk a mile in another person's shoes."

When you're empathetic, you have a genuine care and concern for others that is birthed out of your ability to put yourself in their situation and to feel the feeling they are experiencing at a given moment. It's a fine subtlety, but this definition is what separates empathizers from self-seekers. Empathy is a learned skill that develops through continuous use and practice. While some people are naturally empathetic and can easily feel the pain of others, most of us, find being empathetic challenging.

☯

TAKING THE PRINCIPLE INTO THE MARRIAGE/RELATIONSHIP...

So what can do to improve the level of empathy you have for your spouse? As with the other principles we've discussed so far, with a little practice, you'll become an empathy pro! The first step toward this end begins with focusing on the needs of your partner. Remember, the goal is to put yourself in someone else's position. Fear, anger, frustration, sadness, love, and joy are universal emotions, and it's safe to say that everyone has felt them at one time or another. Tapping into these emotions will help you to identify easily with what your loved one is experiencing and trying to communicate.

Once you tap in, you're halfway there! The next step in developing your empathetic self is actually communicating what you're feeling and thinking to your partner. Communicating the feelings you have tapped into is an extremely effective way to demonstrate your care and concern for someone else. Your ability to communicate empathetically is the key to increasing relational intimacy. It demonstrates to your partner that you are truly concerned about his/her emotional needs. What's more, for those of you who really take increasing your empathy capacity seriously, the time you take investing in the emotional well-being of your loved one will automatically translate into a corresponding action. Before you know it, your relationship will be transformed and you will be experiencing deeper levels of care, commitment, and the other intangibles that come along with this newfound well-spring of emotional intimacy with your partner/spouse.

I'm sure some of you are saying to yourself, "I'm game.... I'll give the empathy challenge a try." However, you just don't know where to start. Well, here are some simple, practical steps to get you on your way.

Step 1: Reserve Judgment & Simply Listen Closely

Do you remember the famous line in the old wine commercial that said, "We will sell no wine before its time"? That's step one in your empathy quest. As you develop empathy skills in your intimate relationships, commit not to make any judgments or develop any opinions about a situation or point of conflict before it's time. And what is the right time? After you've heard your partner out and fully considered his/her perspective and point of view. Empathetic partners listen critically and objectively. That means, while your partner is talking, you suspend all internal dialogue. You know that voice in your head that helps you figure out how to respond to someone while he/she is still talking? Well, put a muzzle on it and give your undivided attention to the person talking. By doing so, you increase your chances of understanding their feelings, and motivations. Also while listening, encourage your partner to continue talking by acknowledging their comments without interrupting.

◉◉

Step 2: Repeat and Reflect What You Heard

Step two calls for you to repeat what you think you heard your partner saying. Be careful during this part of the conversation not to make brush-off comments like "I don't understand why, but I hear you saying that you feel like I..." or "Even though I..." Comments such as these minimize your loved one's feelings and can cause the conversation to head downhill fast!

The safest plan to follow is to simply give them back what they have shared with you. Also, remember to watch your non-verbal cues here. No eye rolling, shoulder shrugging, or distracted looks of disinterest allowed. You are at a critical juncture, and your actions here could determine whether or not your partner ever feels safe and comfortable enough to discuss a sensitive topic with you again. Remember, your goal is to build your relational empathy, not tear your relationship apart. A little care will go a long way toward that end and will cast you in a favorable, sensitive and understanding light to your partner or spouse.

@@

Step 3: Switch Shoes

The last step calls for you to actively engage your imagination and put yourself in your partner's shoes. As a home-school educator and mom, I, Elaine, am always reminding our daughters of the ever-powerful, almost long-forgotten, Golden Rule: "do unto others, as you would have them do unto you." Simply said, treat people the way you want to be treated! This applies to any relationship.

After your partner has shared, ask for a few moments to process what was expressed. As you're processing, ask yourself "What if that was me?" Now, a bit of caution is required here. In response to this question, most people become animated and excited as they describe the things *they* would have done if placed in a similar situation. However, in developing empathy skills, this question is properly addressed by asking yourself a third question, which is "How does/did that make my spouse *feel?*" Asking yourself how your partner feels, makes this question very personal and should help you make the shift from defensive excuses to empathetic understanding. That's empathy in the marriage.

@@

TAKING THE PRINCIPLE INTO THE WORKPLACE...

Empathy in the work place looks a little different and has a slightly different focus. However, the overall goal, "to walk that mile in someone else's shoes," is still the motivation behind developing this emotional skill. Now you might be asking yourself, "What's the point of developing empathy in the workplace?" Well, you'd be surprised how far a little care and understanding can go toward improving working relationships that are key to your success and career.

Utilizing empathy skills in the workplace will demonstrate to your co-workers and team members that you value them as individuals, and not simply for their contribution to the team, which can have a direct correlation to your wallet. As an empathetic leader, you have the ability to develop a high-performing team that demonstrates increased productivity, creativity, morale and commitment to you and your organization. You might be asking yourself how empathy can have so many positive outcomes. The answer is quite simple.

The use of empathy skills in the workplace engenders feelings of safety and comfort. When people feel nurtured, cared for and positively regarded, they naturally become more productive and are more likely to give 110% on their work assignments and duties. The intimacy that is developed in the marriage relationship translates into a sense of team identity in the workplace. Rugged individualism is replaced by a desire to see the best happen for everyone on the team.

Want to transform your work group? Start by investing in the emotional lives of your team members a little at a time. Inquire about their home life, their personal goals, hobbies, and families. If necessary, write down little tidbits to remember about each employee and keep tabs on how things are going in their lives away from the office. Keep in mind that, as we said earlier, we all live only one life. This is why employees' personal problems can affect the morale of the company. If people are having problems at home, one can only expect to have unfocused or distracted employees, because the same problems follow us to our place of work.

These gentle inquiries will communicate your genuine concern for your employees. But, beware, and be sure this technique doesn't backfire on you! Don't make the mistake of confusing the names of one person's children with another person's pets or forget to ask about a really big event your colleague has mentioned to you. Such oversights could undermine all the work you've invested in developing a sense of team and trust amongst your co-workers. Once this ground is lost, it will be nearly impossible to regain. With genuine empathy, these become more than details to remember because you do genuinely care.

If you think you'll have a hard time tapping into the emotions of others and developing the skills needed to become more empathetic, here's a quick and easy way to begin your personal transformation: during a conversation with a co-worker, ask him/her, "How is she/he feeling?" Think about what she/he is talking about and try to see it from his/her perspective. Try to see things from their point of view, even if you disagree. Try to feel what they feel and respond accordingly. Move from the analytical level (thinking) to the emotional (feeling).

Right here, I'd like to offer a word of advice: once you begin developing and utilizing your empathy skills, you may find that some employees or co-workers might not understand, recognize, or adhere to professional boundaries of disclosure and information sharing. At the first sign of an interested party or shoulder to cry on, they may overstep these boundaries and begin dumping all their personal problems on you. Be prepared for these emotionally starved co-workers by gently setting firm boundaries on your time and the things you are willing to discuss in the workplace. Remind them that you share a professional relationship and that while you are definitely interested in their lives outside the office, a little information goes a long way.

Remember, empathy is a matter of the heart and is the result of developing a sincere connection; and in the workplace, a professional connection with others.

❦

Principle 6 Power Points...

- You never truly know someone until you have walked a mile in his/her shoes. Seeking to understand the experiences, circumstances and emotions of others will result in empowered relationships at home and in the workplace.

- "I got shoes, you got shoes, all God's children got shoes!" But, never underestimate the journey your loved-one, coworker, or employee has taken in his or her shoes.

- Make the time to understand the people with whom you interact on a regular basis. Don't assume, presume or conclude. Instead inquire, investigate and elicit. What you discover will help you develop healthy, nurturing, honest and productive relationships

Principle 7: Dream in the Clouds with

Both Feet on the Ground
Set Realistic Expectations

UNDERSTANDING THE PRINCIPLE...

L ove is a wonderful thing! Many songwriters, poets, and artists have spent countless hours singing about, writing about, and creating well known, as well as obscure, expressions of love to, for, and about someone with whom they have or had fallen head over heels in love with. I'm sure you've been there before and experienced the mind-numbing rush that comes with finding that special someone. The giddiness and excitement you experience as you spend time with one another learning likes, dislikes and favorites are all cherished and forever remembered. According to one relational specialist, young couples don't need or demand very much from each other early on in the relationship. These couples spend the majority of their time trying to please one another and expect very little in return. They are simply high on love! There's never enough time in the day, never enough time on the phone, and you can never do enough to please this new god or goddess you have been so fortunate to discover. How in the world were you lucky enough to find Mr. or

Miss. Right? He or she should have been snatched up years ago but the world's loss is another's gain. Right? Right!

However, at some point in the relationship, things begin to change. Marriage and relational specialists have discovered an interesting, if not disturbing, trend. As time passes, each partner's relational needs, desires and expectations change. And if un-addressed, what was once a joyous, fun-loving and fulfilling relationship deteriorates into one of frustration and annoyance. Until newlywed couples enter their second year of marriage, their marital relationship is largely lived based upon false pretenses of one another. During this stage, referred to as the euphoria or honeymoon stage, the fledgling husband and wife team actually interact with each other based upon guise and pretense. They make decisions on how to act, think, respond and interact largely based upon how they believe they will be viewed, interpreted and responded to by their partner. In short, they live their lives based upon false expectations.

What's most unfortunate about this all too common phenomenon is the time wasted by these young couples as they try to live up to the iconic model of a husband or a wife that was either presented to them while growing up, or the role they have cast for themselves. Usually, during this first stage, neither the husband nor the wife possesses enough relational security to share their expectations with their partner. Sad, but true. What's the result? As we stated earlier, this stage generally lasts for a year, at the end of which one of two things happen. Either the couple comes clean with one another about the difficulty each has been having trying to adjust to the rigorous demands of married life or the young couple simply falls into a painful pattern of wedded tedium.

Does any of this sound familiar to you? Have you experienced any of these behaviors in any of your relationships? If you can identify with any of these feelings, experiences or emotions, then consider yourself lucky. One of the major keys to success in any of your current and future relationships is at your fingertips.
Answer these three questions:

- Have you ever been offended or hurt by someone you assumed knew what you thought or expected of him/her?

- Have you ever gotten upset with someone because he/she didn't behave the way you expected him or her to?
- Have you ever found yourself thinking or saying things like: "if you really loved me you would…." why didn't you…." or "I thought you were going to…"; after being surprised, disappointed, or caught off guard by the sentiments or actions of someone else?

Regardless of the relationship type, be it personal or professional, your expectations of friends, loved ones or co-workers have a tremendous impact on how healthy or unhealthy your relationships will be. Unrealistic expectations have been the ruin of many a relationship. So let's examine how they develop.

Unrealistic expectations. The phrase itself gives insight into why they are so damaging and have such a negative impact on our relationships. In general, expectations are the types of behavior that can be reasonably predicted and relied on based upon a person's previously observed habits, skills and abilities, or a person's expression of a desire and willingness to engage in certain new behaviors. Simply put, expectations are a matter of knowing what you will do based on what you have consistently demonstrated. So, if you come home from work and immediately jump in the shower Monday through Friday for three weeks, it is a reasonable and realistic expectation to believe that during week four, you will come straight home from work and jump in the shower. If, for the past 2 years, you have been late to work, without fail, on Friday mornings, there is no reason to expect you to demonstrate any other behavior than that of being late on Friday mornings. This behavior is now a realistic expectation. Sounds simple enough. But where do unrealistic expectations come from and how do we allow them to have such a negative effect on our relationships?

Unrealistic expectations are based upon perceived patterns of behavior that substitute the ideal, for the real, and are usually based upon romantically fantasized notions of what a relationship is supposed to look and feel like. Many times, we develop relational expectations long before we meet the man or woman upon whom we will super-impose and task them with making us happy. Now that's not an intelligent approach to creating long-lasting healthy relationships. Invariably, unrealistic expectations are connected, to varying degrees, to issues of power, manipulation and control. When you develop and harbor impossible expectations for your partner to meet, you become blinded and closed to discovering and understanding who he/she really is. To compound matters, even if your partner tries to live up to your expectations, he or she will never be able to do so. Why? It is because relational expectations are usually highly unattainable and, are not based upon the actual strengths of our partners.

Taking the Principle into the Marriage/Relationship...

By now, I'm sure you're aware that I, Elaine, am the bona-fide Type B personality. I'm more laid-back, easygoing, and analytical, yet very observant and in-tune emotionally. As a wife and mother, I naturally wear a number of hats, and my responsibilities vary from day to day. I also home school our five daughters, which means that the number of hats is increased by ten! {I know, it makes you tired just thinking about it!} Thus, not only am I wife and mother, but also I'm also a teacher, a nurse, a counselor, referee, coach, lunch lady and school principal! Even on a non-working day, I'm working. Now, there have been times when Eric has called home and asked me to make a phone call to a client or work on a particular project, and the phone call wasn't made or the project wasn't complete for some unknown reason, right? Well, after numerous discussions that were sometimes of a high pitch nature (to put it mildly!), what we both agreed to do was to pick up the pace on my end and to slow down the time frame of expectancy on his end. We've learned and are continuing to learn to set realistic expectations with one another.

Now let's explore how to go about avoiding setting and operating on unrealistic expectations in our personal relationship. The first step involves working with what you were given. A simple way to monitor relational factors is summed up in the ideal that warns us not to expect what you do not inspect. What does this mean? It means that one should not require without taking into consideration numerous factors that will contribute or affect the fulfillment of the request. Understanding the need as well as the potential of your spouse will contribute to the progress and health of the relationship. (Elaine speaking) For instance, Eric and I are fully aware of our potential to do *anything* we put our minds to. Yet, it is when we are given the opportunity to flow in our *element* that we operate as a well-oiled machine. However, unrealistic expectations are inevitable if left un-addressed and un-agreed upon by both parties.

Expectations with another person are useful only when verbalized. Taking the time to learn and inspect what each person's strengths and natural abilities are and the reasonable timeframe of expectancy will go a long way toward ensuring that no feelings are hurt and that no expectations will go unmet.

Always recognize and operate based upon a realistic understanding of what you want, what you will accept and what your partner is able and willing to contribute to the relationship. Taking the time to clearly define each of these categories will allow you to create realistic goals for your relationship based on solid and healthy expectations. It is great to set high expectations for your relationship, as long as these expectations are based in the reality of you and your partner's abilities and desires. These activities are generally ignored by overly-confident couples who hold to the hope and unfounded belief that love, alone, will make a way for their relationship to survive. But, let's be practical. If you can't swim, don't jump into the deep end of the pool. If you aren't good in math, don't apply for a job as an accountant and, lastly, don't look for your recluse of a husband to take you out *every* Friday night. Live in the real, not the ideal.

Another key to overcoming or avoiding unrealistic relational expectations is finding what we refer to as "grieve it" or "get it." Who says your partner or spouse is supposed to meet every relational/emotional need you have? If, after you've expressed your expectations and the two of you have mutually agreed that your partner or spouse just isn't able to deliver in that area, be willing to empower yourself and find ways to meet your own needs. Need more excitement and adventure but you're married to a homebody? With your partner's approval and support, have a regularly scheduled girl's night out or guy's night out to scratch that social itch. Sometimes, invest in your relationship with your "homebody" by renting movies and cuddling on the couch at home where he/she is most comfortable and content. On the flip side, you must also be willing to let go of some of your must-have expectations for the sake of your relationship. Don't pout, get angry, or find passive-aggressive ways to retaliate once you realize your spouse either can't or won't meet your relational expectations. Instead, allow yourself to grieve the sacrifices that go along with being in a committed relationship. Don't allow the perceived need to have your list of expectations, realistic or otherwise, met by your partner.

Instead, override this need with the joy of being in a relationship with someone who cares enough to try to make the adjustments needed to increase your chances of happiness. Accepting your partner and the life you can have, together, is the key to a long-term, happy, healthy relationship in marriage. Sow into the relationship what you want to receive and it will be given back to you.

@@

Taking the Principle into the Workplace...

In terms of unrealistic expectations and their impact in the workplace, many of the sentiments already mentioned apply. However, especially if you oversee people in the workplace, the method required is slightly different. By and large, in this, the age of learning organizations, high performance teams, total quality management and organizational development, it is very difficult for an employee or manager to operate based upon faulty or unrealistic expectations. However, for whatever reasons, some problems may persist. In order to deal with these problems, utilize the keys mentioned above to ward off frustration, poor job performance, criticism and outright animosity in the workplace.

When dealing with your employees or team members, always remember that, when it comes to communication and addressing unrealistic expectations, more is better. Patiently take the time to determine each person's job assignment, duties, and performance measures from day one. Leave little room for guesswork. You never want an employee to be caught off guard by an evaluation or performance appraisal. As such, an open door policy, frequent team meetings and informal one-on-one get-togethers where you simply discuss how things are going for each team member will go a long way toward preventing the development, or perpetuation of unrealistic expectations.

But, what happens when something is brought to your attention? How do you handle an employee's or team member's unrealistic expectations? In short, you address it one-on-one, head on. Meet with the person and inquire as to why and how she/he developed the unrealistic expectation. The misunderstanding could be the result of faulty communication, a misunderstanding, or any number of innocent issues. Once expressed, set the record straight by providing your colleague a clear understanding of what is expected of him/her and ensure the unrealistic expectation has been addressed and replaced with a much clearer and appropriate one.

Disappointment, frustration and disillusionment in relationships almost invariably stem from unmet and perhaps unrealistic expectations of what a relationship should look like. In order to avoid them, take some time to assess what you expect to get from both your personal and professional relationships. Ask yourself hard questions regarding what you expect and what you allow others to expect from you, both at home and at the office. By doing so, you will build healthy, empowered and honest relationships that provide support and comfort as opposed to stress and continual disappointment. Put in the work, and you'll reap the reward.

☯

Principle 7 Power Points…

- No one starts out as a master or an expert in anything – education and experiences, along the way, shape each of us to be this way. Allow for a period of growth in working with others and be patient with their progress and development. How patient? As patient as you'd like others to be with you.

- Human nature causes us to interact with family, friends, loved ones, and even co-workers based upon expectations. Clearly stated and agreed upon expectations can result in the development of more deeply meaningful and honest relationships. However, when left unspoken, these same expectations become deadly obstacles to relational intimacy and professional trust.

- The key to discovering and overturning unrealistic relational expectations is honest communication. Share your expectations with your partner or colleagues. Don't hide from the conflict that may ensue; instead use it to increase your interpersonal intimate and workplace connections.

Principle 8: Feel It Through

Learn to Resolve Conflict
in a Healthy Way

UNDERSTANDING THE PRINCIPLE...

Conflict... there's a concept we're all familiar with! Since the beginning of time, every being has experienced conflict with another. All you need is two people, two animals, two insects – two anything – and eventually, there will be conflict. When discussing conflict, we cannot talk about eliminating it. As we have learned, conflict simply exists. We learn to manage and resolve it in a healthy way.

What is the nature of conflict? Conflict occurs when two different people with two different wills interact and one of them desires to impose his or her will, preference, or way over the other – but the other ain't having it! Thus, a battle begins, and the winner of the battle will determine which individual's will or preference will triumph over the other. The more we feel we have to lose, the harder we fight. The more our opponent seems to be weakening, the more forceful we become. We don't mean any harm. We just want our way this time. And maybe next time, too.

The key to winning when it comes to interpersonal relationships and conflict is twofold: 1) not dominating your partner. 2) understanding that when differences arise in what you want versus what they want, a workable, win-win agreement can be found. The goal is for everyone to walk away feeling heard, valued and respected. These are people you love and respect, remember? That doesn't mean that everyone will have their way but they will, at least, feel like the compromise was fair. This is called healthy conflict resolution.

Can conflict really be healthy? You bet! You see, it's not avoiding conflict that can build an interpersonal relationship, it's about how the two people who are involved negotiate the cause of the conflict. If they can resolve it with respect and courtesy, instead of having either feeling emotionally bruised or beaten down, then the relationship can heal and grow stronger than it was before they engaged in the conflict. This means that conflict can actually be a good thing! Who knew?

In spite of this, you're always going to have people who avoid conflict because they want to keep the peace and hold things together. Avoidance doesn't benefit anything, including the relationship. If you avoid conflict, you are simply robbing your relationship of the opportunity to grow and develop in ways that can only occur when you sit down with another and patiently, rationally work through your issues. Further, avoidance means that issues can exist between you for extended periods of time without ever being dealt with. Is this what you want?

Our point is, avoiding conflict is very bad, however, dealing with it properly can be very healthy – the best thing to happen to you and your relationship. Since our goal is to help you have healthy interpersonal relationships, then we are in favor of showing you how to handle conflict properly.

TAKING THE PRINCIPLE TO THE MARRIAGE/RELATIONSHIP...

You and your partner don't need for us to tell you that when you are in a relationship, you will have conflict. In fact, you may have already had some conflict today before you began reading this chapter. We don't know how you dealt with this conflict, but hopefully, after reading this chapter, you will be better equipped to deal with it in a way that both of you will feel like winners. However, the only way you can both feel like winners is to fight fair.

The very word "fair" implies that there is a set of standards or rules that are not to be violated. Any behavior that falls within these rules or standards is considered acceptable, "fair" behavior. Anything that violates the rules or standards in any way is considered unacceptable and "unfair." If the both spouses involved in a conflict are not able to agree on a set of standards or rules that will serve as parameters for their conflict resolution, they are doomed from the beginning. Most couples, though, are willing to, at least, agree on the need for some ground rules for fair discussions. Remember, you love one another and you want to see things work out. No one, typically, starts out wanting the relationship to end.

When you disagree, which is inevitable, you must fight fair. There are some things which are forbidden and completely off limits for you to think, say, and do to your partner during these heated exchanges. Here are some tips on how to fight fair that every couple must know.

Tip 1: Take Your Time and Watch Your Words

The old saying that we used to sing on the playground to the mean kids who insulted us goes, "Sticks and stones can break my bones, but words can never hurt me!" How wrong we were! Words are powerful. They can either build up a person or they can tear down and utterly destroy someone. Much of the pain, resentment, lack of forgiveness and wounds to the soul that people carry are a result of the words spoken to them by the very people they loved and trusted. Sometimes physical blows cause this pain. Most often, the things that make it difficult to have high self-esteem, self-confidence, and belief in ourselves and our ability to do or be anything are a direct result of words spoken to us. "You're ugly!" "You're stupid!" "You'll never be anything in life!" "No one will ever want you!" "I hate that you were ever born!" "You can't do anything right!" Sticks and stones can cause physical harm, right? Definitely! Over time, these physical wounds may heal; but words from someone you love can injure your very soul for the rest of your life.

When we are wounded by words, it is rarely from a stranger. The wound is almost always from someone who we love and trust. Someone we thought would protect us. Someone we thought would always have our back, tell us the truth, and defend us from the rest of the world. This is what makes the words hurt the most – the fact that the hurt and betrayal came from your closest allies inside the camp, rather than from the outside. You now, no longer know if you should feel accepted or rejected. You are also grappling with feelings of vulnerability and you are definitely on the defensive with the very people that you once felt loved and protected by.

Think about it. If a stranger walks up to you while you're waiting in line to get coffee and says, "You destroy everything you touch in your life," and then walks away, your initial thought is "Who is this guy? He doesn't know me. He must have me mistaken with someone else. He doesn't know anything about what I do or how good I am at it. That guy's crazy!" With this, we dismiss his words, chalk it up to a crazy encounter in the coffee line and file it away as a story to tell later to friends at lunch. The words of a stranger don't hurt because you have no reason to trust his/her assessment.

Now, let's flip the scenario and make it an encounter with someone you respect, love and trust. This is someone who knows you, your history, your vulnerabilities, and your issues. While you are standing in the coffee line with them, if they are silent for a few moments, before turning, to look at you with a serious expression to say, "You know, you destroy everything you touch in your life."

Instantly, you feel like you've been punched in the stomach. In fact, you might double over as a result of the physical and emotional pain you feel, but instead you choose to stand upright and keep your composure because you're in the middle of a busy coffee house. The first question you ask in this scenario is, "Why do you say that?" This person is close enough to you to have an accurate read of your life, so if he/she said it, it could be true – and now you want the evidence. You may not have seen it their way before, and after he/she explains it, you may not see it their way afterwards, but it is a painful truth to hear, nonetheless. Days, months, even years after the exchange, you remember these words. They replay over and over in your mind, and they impact the decisions you make, the way you deal with others, and the way you feel about yourself and your ability to have successful relationships. Our point here: strangers can't hurt you with words like a loved one can, and this hurt is not just for the moment, it's for a lifetime.

You see, the thing about words is that they never go away. If the wrong words come out of your mouth and enter your partner's hearing, you can never, ever, ever take them back. When you use words as a tool to hurt your spouse, he/she will never understand how you allowed yourself to say such things to him or her. Yes, they know that you were in the heat of the moment. Yes, they know that you were simply being passionate and you were just trying to make a point; but there's an underlying truth that says: "out of the abundance of the heart, the mouth speaks." This means that even though you said it by accident, in the heat of the moment, when you were less careful about what was coming out of your mouth, you meant it. Obviously, what was hidden in your heart all along came out.

Have you ever let a set of words, an opinion, or an accusation slip out of your mouth during an intense argument with your partner? Just when you thought you were losing, you decided to pull out the big guns (symbolically speaking). You knew that these would be the words that would shock them. Stun them. End the argument instantly. You were trying not to go there but, now, because your partner wouldn't listen; wouldn't say you were right; or wouldn't give you your way; you decide to say hurtful words to them. As soon as they escaped your lips, you wished that you could give your very life to take them back so that you wouldn't have to see that deep, intense hurt that you just inflicted on your partner – your soul mate for life. The one you love.

Here's the other thing that you should know. Saying, "I'm sorry" is never enough. It's kind of like we've been trained to look at our partner's face, and at that moment when great disappointment is written all over it, we have an internal reflex that is activated to say, "I'm sorry." You know, people tend to think that "I'm sorry" works like those nifty little magic erasers you find in the store. I can say whatever I want to say, and if it hurts you to the point that it makes me feel guilty, I can erase everything – my irresponsible words, your hurt, and most of all, my guilt – by simply uttering two little words. "I'm sorry" is so ineffective in such circumstances that you might as well keep the words to yourself for the time being.

Our point in all of this is that when you are engaged in conflict with your partner; don't let the passion and intensity get the best of you. Calm down and watch your words because they have power and you can never take them back. Don't just spout off at the mouth! Before you *say* it, *think* about it. Even if it seems like it *might* be the wrong thing to say, don't say it all! The wrong words spoken at the wrong time over the years can tear down your partner – word by word – and literally destroy your marriage. You must be very careful and intentional with the words you use, because even though you desire to win the fight; to get your way or to make your point with your partner, it's not worth inflicting pain on them that lasts for the rest of their lives. And it's not worth seeing your relationship go down the drain.

❧

Tip 2: Put Yourself in Your Spouse's Shoes

If you recall reading the principle at the top of this chapter, it said "Feel It Through." When we talk about putting yourself in your partner's shoes, this is exactly what we are talking about. Another fancier word for it is empathy, as discussed previously, which is simply understanding another's emotions and being able to enter into or share what they might be feeling. Empathy is a critical component of what makes societies around the world function. Without it, we would encounter mindless acts of evil, violence, and terror on a daily basis. Having the ability to put yourself in someone else's shoes and predict the hurt it could potentially cause them allows you to avoid engaging in behaviors that will harm them. You feel their potential pain that could result from your actions and you decide not to inflict it upon them. Empathy asks, "How would this make them feel?"

When it comes to conflict with your spouse, we want you to *feel it through*. We know that we just finished discussing how to fight fair because we know that in some instances, you will, indeed, verbally fight! However, empathy is necessary for you to even have the ability to fight fair. In putting yourself in your partner's shoes and predicting how your words will make them feel, you are exercising empathy already. This tip is simply about taking that empathy to the next level.

Feeling it through instead of fighting it out refers to the need for you and your spouse to sit down and sincerely understand the impact of how conflict is making each of you feel. Too often, we suppress the way we feel to make our spouse happy. Remember, this behavior is not healthy for a relationship because, eventually, tempers are going to blow up – usually at the wrong time. Don't suppress the way you feel about a topic of conflict. Don't save it for later so that you can address multiple issues at once. "Feeling it through" is about, truthfully, acknowledging how you feel about the matter to yourself and then being prepared to share these feelings with your spouse in order to come to the best resolution for the relationship and the family.

"Feeling it through" is not about having a shouting match or seeing who can be the loudest to get their way. It's not even about who can present the most logical argument in a calm manner. No, this tip has a different focus. It is where the both partners sit down and ask, "I feel one way and you feel another way, but which way is best for our relationship and our family?" You are now engaged in feeling one another because you both have the same goal in mind: a happy, healthy, functional family.

When you "feel it through" instead of fighting it out, you are acknowledging that it does your relationship no good for one of you to get your way while you, both, have an unhappy home. What good does that do? The goal is mutual fulfillment. Mutual gratification. Doing what's best for "us" rather than what's best for "me". When two partners have the maturity to "feel it through", their relationship wins. When they resolve their conflict by letting the louder, stronger, more insistent partner have his or her way, the relationship becomes a ticking time bomb because the losing partner will only live so long like this before blowing up and blowing out!

Now, keep in mind, we *are* talking about conflict, so "feeling it through" in the midst of frustration won't be easy! When faced with a conflict, it might be best to step away and give each other the space to gather your head; think soberly before coming together to discuss it. Healthy conflict resolution takes care and intention, and both of these take time!

Tip 3: It's Okay to Use a Mediator

Some conflicts are easier to resolve than others. Whether we're going to start buying whole wheat bread instead of white might be resolved in a few minutes. Whether we're going to spend our savings on a new set of golf clubs may take a few hours. Whether we're going to go to my family's home for Thanksgiving or your family's home might be resolved in one weekend. Whether we're going to buy a sedan or a minivan might be resolved in one week. These are considered minor issues in which you must make the decision to either wrestle or rest. Some things are not detrimental enough to really wrestle with in your head, so you can allow these things to simply rest. They're not a major issue.

And then there are those issues that seem like they could take a lifetime to work out such as:

- Whether we can sacrifice for you to be a stay-at-home mom
- Whether you must go to work to help with the bills
- Whether to allow our child to pick her own religion
- Whether our marriage can survive with your bossy mother living with us
- Whether you *control* the money in the house and we give me an allowance or we both have access to the account
- Whether I should be angry that you took it upon yourself to take out an equity loan on the house without telling me.

Issues this important can become major deal breakers because they can very well make or break a relationship. These are the kind of issues that tend to be ongoing conflicts, you know, like the ones you think you've resolved for good until the other spouse can't take living with the resolution anymore and brings it up again. The content spouse thought it was resolved all along, when, in fact, it wasn't resting well with the other spouse – he or she was just going along with the plan. The resolution probably came as a result of one spouse yielding to the agreement because he or she was tired of fighting about it, because it was doing too much damage to the relationship or because there didn't seem to be any other option except for someone to, finally, give in. When this occurs, the conflict has not been properly dealt with. For issues this major, you might need a little help.

Help is not a bad thing; it's a great thing! There are two hurdles that a couple must get over, however, in order to pursue help: social stigma and pride. First, you'll have to get over the social stigma of "help" because when people hear that you are getting help, they automatically start the buzz: "Is their marriage in trouble?" or "I told you one of them was crazy. Now we *know* it's true!" People are always interested in other people's marriages. In reality, judging from the divorce rate, most of the people around you are in more troubled marriages than you. They'd rather roll the dice to see how things turn out than get help. That's quite a gamble. The second thing that you'll have to get over is the issue of pride. Some spouses are so private that they are not willing to share their "personal business" with anyone else, even if another person can help them. Why? Because they believe that any admission of being less than perfect or having a less than perfect marriage will make them look bad. They'd rather *look* good than actually *have* a good marriage. Question: how good will you look standing before the judge in divorce court because you refused to get help? Another issue with a proud spouse is that rather than openly disclose details of their relationship, he/she'd rather suffer in silence and eventually walk away from the marriage – all because of pride. Our advice to the proud: focus on what's important. Looking good *is not* important. Having a good marriage *is* important. Looking *like* the ideal family *is not* important. *Being* the ideal family *is* important. Remember: pride comes before destruction!

If you are going to be a healthy, functional couple that is genuinely interested in healthy conflict resolution, you should always have a non-biased third party that you can go to when you and your spouse are unable to resolve an issue yourselves. When we say non-biased, we mean someone who has no vested interested in your relationship and who has nothing to gain from declaring either you or your spouse the victor in any conflict you bring his/her way. Now, when you search for a non-biased third party, this person should be someone who shares the belief system and values that you and your spouse share, so that when he/she makes a judgment call, it is in a direction that will not cause you to violate your principles. A good example of whom a third party might be is a pastor, rabbi, minister, mentor, professional counselor, psychologist or a well-experienced – seasoned in age/maturity – mutual friend who has the best interest of your relationship or marriage at heart.

When you submit yourselves to this non-biased third party, however, there is one rule that you and your spouse must observe: whatever they say has to be the law of the land – the last say-so... the final authority! If your advisor rules in the direction opposite of your conviction, you have to be willing and mature enough to accept his/her decision, follow their guidance, and do it gladly without complaining or skepticism – no matter how right you are convinced you are. You can't ask for a second opinion from someone else after things do not go your way! The outcome stands once and for all, and that's that. It's the only way the conflict can be resolved.

TAKING THE PRINCIPLE TO THE WORKPLACE...

Discussing conflict in the workplace can get trickier. The people in the workplace are neither committed to you, nor committed to any particular unifying set of values. They are committed to one thing in the workplace; money which motivates them to get up, get dressed, fight traffic, paste on fake smiles and report for work everyday. The job to helps them finance their families and their lifestyles. Their purposes, then, are self-focused and if you get in the way of or threaten their purpose in any way, there's going to be conflict – and they'll be out to win.

This being said, the same rules do not necessarily apply to the workplace as in the marriage, yet there are some similarities. Even though you may play by one set of rules (the fair ones that you've learned in reading this book), your co-workers may play by a completely different set of rules or even, rules with no boundaries. They will say whatever they have to say, do whatever they have to do, and go wherever they have to go in order to win the conflict and keep their job. Their passion even goes to a different level because when you threaten them in the workplace, you are threatening their paycheck, which is their very survival; for this reason, when there is conflict in the workplace, it can get quite serious.

The fact that everyone doesn't play by the same rules in the workplace doesn't mean that you cannot resolve conflict in a healthy way. Remember, most of the principles that we've learned are universal, meaning they can be used in any area of life. Thus, instead of presenting you with a completely new set of tips for healthy conflict resolution in the workplace, we'll tell you how you can adapt the ones you've already learned.

Tip 1: Take Your Time and Watch Your Words

Just like in the marriage, people in the workplace never forget what you say. It's almost as if co-workers build up a mental file on you so that they can come back and use it at the least opportune time in the future to sabotage you. This is the best reason to watch your words in the midst of conflict. Whether you are engaging in conflict with an office friend or foe, say only what needs to be said; state facts not opinions. And, for heaven's sake, don't call names, make accusations, or speak negatively about anyone in the office!

Unfortunately, while a personal relationship is characterized by love, the workplace is a little more ruthless. It's all about the survival of the fittest when it comes to engaging in conflict in the workplace. In most instances, co-workers are not out to see the company win! They are, ultimately, out to see themselves win so that they can shine in front of the boss, keep their jobs and maintain their livelihood. This is good reason to stay calm in a conflict, deal with the facts, restrain yourself from voicing any negative opinions and keep your composure. *Watch your words!* In the marriage, you can hurt your spouse with words during conflict. In the workplace, you can give your co-workers ammunition for the future - for everything you say will eventually be used against you.

❦

Tip 2: Put Yourself in Your Co-Worker's Shoes

Here, we are referring to having empathy for your business partner or co-worker. Although you need to be on guard when a conflict arises in the workplace, you still gotta have a heart! After all, you can't allow the workplace to strip you of your values and ethics, can you? Developing empathy for the person with whom you are engaged in conflict will help you become more effective at resolving workplace conflict. And it will also make you an office favorite.

When co-workers engage in conflict, there are two differing perspectives about how something should be done – you don't see eye to eye. Instead of charging ahead and trying to impose your will on another, take a different approach by just listening, first. Allow yourself to be mature and sincere enough to try to see the other point of view. Why is he/she so dedicated to their point of view? What outcome is she expecting to occur? How is this making him feel? Does your opposing perspective threaten him/her in any way? Take an inventory of all these possibilities. Then deal with them – sincerely – from this vantage point. If these questions express a belief or an attempt, it allows the other to share. If we say we "understand" or "can see" this might seem patronizing. Start with, "I believe I understand how you feel…" and "I'm trying to see your point about how this will…" You'll be amazed at how disarming this approach will be and how much of an impact it will have on his/her willingness to discuss the best option rather than forcing their will.

Many times, when people are very forceful, aggressive, and insistent on having their way, they are operating out of fear, which may include: fear of losing control of the situation or the environment; fear of losing a certain image or status that they think is critical to maintaining their position; and fear of losing the job position itself. Yes, the workplace can be the proverbial jungle. However, with some patience and intentionality, you can turn most every workplace foe into a friend.

Tip 3: Remove the Filters

Filters are protective screens that cause distortion in what is heard. Filters are good for keeping our cars and appliances working well, by preventing the bad junk from getting into the engine or motor and such. However, filters are bad for relationships. As humans with different experiences, pasts and backgrounds our filters, oftentimes, *keep the bad* and *wash away the good*. It's human nature, it seems. As we've shared, we are all products of genetics (nature) and our upbringing (nurture). So many of us have never experienced nor seen modeled before us what it looks like to fight fair. Because of our background, childhood history and past relationships and experiences, we tend to hear things or respond to situations through a filter. Remove the filters and experience things for the way they really are. **(Elaine speaking) Eric and I have learned to recognize when we've 'installed' our filter and we laugh about it, now. But, our filter use was not always a laughing matter.**

◎◎

Tip 4: It's Okay to Use a Mediator!

While the options for a third party mediator are different in the workplace than in the marriage, the concept is still the same. Some issues can be worked out by having a calm, rational conversation with your co-workers. Other issues, especially those that are on going, might require some assistance in order to be resolved once and for all. In the workplace, you have access to specialists who are trained in helping you negotiate fair resolutions, like an ombudsman or a human resources representative. Higher-level managers often have some training in this skill as well. If you don't want the conflict to go on the official record at the company, you and your co-worker might also choose to use a trusted, respected mentor in the workplace who can help you come to a resolution. Whoever you decide to use, the most important response is to get help when you can't work things out yourselves.

The same resistance to getting help to resolve conflict in a marriage will appear right before your very eyes in the workplace: social stigma and pride! Likewise, similar approaches to get over these in the marriage also work for the workplace. If you want the conflict resolved once and for all, seek a fair, objective third-party who can do wonders for helping you to resolve a problem.

I (Elaine) had the privilege of learning a very important lesson about conflict at my first job, which I secured with Daniel Radiator when I was 16 years old. I quickly worked my way up from an inventory file clerk to a receptionist position, which I loved (Type B personality and baby of the family – people person)! One day, I

104

remember sitting at the front desk and watching two of the company's top executives have a knock-out, drag-out — a loud confrontational disagreement on how an account was being handled. I remembered feeling uneasy, a little scared and ready to hit the three magic buttons on the telephone: 9-1-1!

However, shortly after their 5-minute explosion, the Vice President turned to the company Comptroller as he grabbed his jacket and said, "Okay, so where are we going for lunch?" I was just amazed as I gasped for air and was finally able to breathe a sigh of relief. It was on this day that I learned a valuable, life-changing lesson: I learned that conflict is not a bad thing. It doesn't mean the end of the world as I grew up believing that it would. They taught me that you could still be friends and have disagreements, as long as you fight fair. Allow each other to speak their heart, feel what you feel ("feel it through"), make the necessary adjustments and just move on!

Like the marriage, try not to avoid conflict resolution in the workplace. Remember, if you have two people together in the same setting, eventually and inevitably, there will be some conflict. It's not avoidance of conflict that makes the workplace enjoyable; it's the healthy resolution of it. When you learn how to resolve conflict in a healthy manner in the workplace, you will be well-respected among your peers, seen favorably by your managers and bosses, and on your way to managing other people. Why? Because the skill of being able to help people resolve conflict is one of the most essential skills a manager can have.

Principle 8 Power Points…

- Engaging in behaviors such as yelling, name-calling, and insulting gets you nowhere in the midst of a heated conflict. These tactics only breed resentment, paranoia and confusion that ultimately keep you from accomplishing your mutual goals.

- Allow people the time and distance to work through their issues and then come together to work on the issue as a team.

- When you learn to resolve conflict in the workplace, it strengthens your negotiation skills and people will like and trust you more than others in the office!

- Allow each other to speak their heart, feel what you feel (feel it through), make the necessary adjustments and just move on!

Principle 9: You're Not "All that" by Yourself

Learn, Discover, and Utilize the Strengths of Others

UNDERSTANDING THE PRINCIPLE...

Back in the day, when our parents' were young and thought they were the best at something, they would say they were "the rat, the cheese, and the smell." In our teen years, we said we were "too-legit-to-quit" or "all that plus a bag of chips". Today, the young people say that they're "the stuff". So, as we've journeyed down memory lane of cliché's we've titled this chapter, you're *not* "all that" by yourself! If you have self-esteem and self-confidence, it's not unhealthy to consider yourself to be one of the best. You may have heard the saying, "It's a poor dog that can't wag its own tail." Many people have already gotten this concept. The harm is not in thinking that you're the greatest; the problem comes in when you can only see the value in yourself to the extent that you can no longer see it in other people.

When you neglect the gifts, talents or contributions of others you rob yourself of a lot. People who think that they have everything to offer and that others have very little to offer often begin to exude a sense of pride and arrogance which doesn't look good. The arrogance can be so strong that people can recognize it as soon as they meet such a person because it goes beyond confidence. It's more like confidence out of control!

People who think they are "all that" often overlook the fact that it took the contributions of others to get them where they are today. In fact, these individuals tend to take full credit for where they are, considering themselves to be self-made. In their minds, they got where they are as a result of their hard work, determination, the way they think and the way they achieve a goal, etc. As a result, people who think they are "all that" can be very difficult to coach. Have you ever tried giving advice to people like this? If so, you probably walked away shaking your head and muttering, "Know it all."

Nobody likes to be in a relationship with someone who always takes all of the credit. Everybody wants to feel valued and important, like they are making a contribution to the team. Ahh... there's a concept! Team. You see, that's what this lesson is all about. Whenever you are engaged in a relationship with someone with whom you are trying to work together to achieve a common goal, you've got to have two people who are willing to learn, discover, and utilize the strengths of each other in order to accomplish that goal. It simply won't work if one of the people thinks he or she is "all that," because this attitude will not make for a workable relationship. God forbid if both people think that they are "all that", because a train wreck is on the way!

Many relationships fail both at home and in the workplace because of a know-it-all attitude. One person in the party designates him/herself to be the authority on everything, virtually silencing the voices of the other player or players on the team. While it is true that the team may win, every player wants to feel like he made a contribution. No one with a healthy self-esteem simply wants to go along with the ride. It is simply a part of human nature to feel a sense of being needed... and wanted.

TAKING THE PRINCIPLE TO THE BEDROOM...

Anytime more than one person works together to accomplish a common goal, they become a team which includes a marital or romantic relationship. Both spouses represent the two people working together toward the common goal, and the goal is to build and maintain a healthy, successful relationship in which both are mutually satisfied.

Mutual satisfaction is not something that occurs accidentally. It is not the result of passive behavior in a relationship. At the end of the day, in order for both spouses to walk away saying, "Yes, I'm satisfied," both people had to work carefully and intentionally to ensure that their partner's needs were met. However, remember that people need to feel needed and wanted. Perhaps this is one of the primary reasons that millions of people in troubled marriages report that they are not satisfied.

Ask yourself these questions: "Can my spouse make it without me?" "Does my spouse profess to do everything better than me?" "Does my spouse seek out my advice or find my input valuable when decisions need to be made?" "Does my spouse seem to disapprove and criticize everything I do and the way I think?" "Am I left feeling inadequate after relating to my spouse?"

If you are feeling discontented in your relationship, taking the time to make this evaluation may unlock some key reasons behind your discontentment. Perhaps you are already consciously aware of your partner's disregard for you and your intellectual and physical contributions to the relationship. Have you already shut down and withdrawn from the relationship because you feel insignificant? Do you feel yourself unsatisfied and headed that way?

Elaine and I may not be addressing a problem that you are dealing with in your marriage. If we are not, keep reading – you may be able to help a friend with this one day. There is also a possibility that we *are* addressing you, the partner who thinks that he or she is "all that." Again, keep on reading, and perhaps by the end of this chapter, you will have a higher regard for what other people can offer you – as a person who knows everything and can do anything.

If we leave both partners with one key piece of advice on this principle, it is: everyone has strengths, regardless of where they're from, what they've been through, what they look like, how much money or education they have or how passive they are. Strengths can be so subtle and manifest themselves in so many different ways that you may not realize that they are strengths. If you can look at your partner and honestly say that she or he does not have any strengths, skills or talents to contribute to your relationship, your vision is off.

Want to know what the real deal is? Value. It's not that your partner does not have any strengths, skills, or talents. You know that they exist. The truth is that you do not value what your spouse brings to the relationship because you've allowed all of the greatness that you bring to overshadow your partner. You've decided that you are "all that", and as a result, you've excluded your spouse. Guess what happens to people who feel like they're not needed and insignificant, while the other spouse handles everything "the right way"? You got it. They eventually leave in pursuit of a relationship where they feel wanted, needed, and significant. Remember: to feel needed and significant are basic human *needs*, not wants.

Here's some breaking news: if your marriage or relationship is making it, you're not making it alone. No matter what it looks like, you're not doing this all by yourself! While it looks like you are holding up this partnership single-handedly, your spouse is making valuable contributions to keep things going, even though you might not consider them valuable. What a lonely place to be for someone who loves you. Don't despair; all hope is not lost. With a few intentional efforts, you can change this.

What does it take to learn, discover, and utilize the strengths of others? If doing this is difficult for you, we'd like to give you a few tips that will help.

☠

Tip 1: Humble Yourself

In order to get where you want to go, here, you're going to need to take a few steps back and humble yourself. You're going to need to tell yourself, "I am not "all that by myself," and further, you must *mean* it (going through the motions does no good if you aren't sincere). After you say this to yourself, then tell yourself why. Review your history and note all of the ways people have helped you in the past. Acknowledge your flaws and your shortcomings by taking a personal inventory. Next, tell yourself, "I am not responsible for everything good that happens in this relationship and this household," and again, mean it.

By the end of this exercise, you should now realize that your success wasn't all you and you really aren't "all that by yourself."

◎◉◎

Tip 2: Do An Inventory on Your Spouse

After you have done the inventory on yourself, get out a pencil and a sheet of paper (not a little one, a big one – you'll need more than you think!) and challenge yourself to list every positive attribute, every good quality, and every strength that your spouse possesses. If you get stalled as soon as you get started, go back to what you used to think were positive attributes, good qualities, and strengths in the past. Go back to when you first met. Go back to when your partner was there for you during a challenging time in your life. Go back to when you remember your spouse being there for someone else who was going through a difficult time. Think back to those moments when you were most proud of your spouse in the past. Reflect back on what people used to say (or currently say) when they give your spouse compliments, and when you stand at your spouse's side in proud agreement.

By the end of this exercise, you should have reminded yourself about all of the great strengths and qualities that your partner possesses, and it should be clear, at this point, that the problem was not your partner's lack of strength, but your old perspective.

◎◉◎

Tip 3: Take Time to Imagine

The next step is an imagination exercise. It should be fun. After you read the instructions for this tip, close your eyes and imagine what life would be like without the contributions your spouse makes on a daily basis. Start with seeing yourself waking up on Monday morning, and track the progress of the day all the way through bedtime. Leave no stone unturned. Where would you be able to live? What would you eat? Where would you get money? Who would care for the children? Would you feel safe and secure? Would you feel lonely? Who would you watch your favorite shows with? Who knows you well enough to offer sound advice? Who would manage each aspect of the household?

By the end of this exercise, you should recognize the numerous contributions that your spouse makes, both tangible and intangible. Sometimes, you can measure your partner's contributions by how much time they spend doing something or their level of commitment; and sometimes your spouses contributions are less measurable – things like their presence by your side when you are nervous, their ability to calm you down when you get really angry, the way they can comfort you and your children like no one else can, the sense of security you feel when they are near, or even how they can make you feel loved like no one else in the world. Your spouse's contributions may be very different from yours, but that does not make them any less significant.

◎◎

Tip 4: Genuinely Appreciate Your Spouse

In case you haven't caught on already, we're going somewhere here. All of the previous assessments were simply leading you to see your spouse with fresh eyes. What you should have taken away from the exercises is that your spouse has made valuable contributions to who you are and what you have been able to accomplish (if you've been together for any length of time).

In light of this, it's time to appreciate your spouse. He or she may not be everything you'd like for a partner to be, but hey, who's perfect? Our partners are our teammates, and they've probably contributed a whole lot more to our happiness and success than we've given them credit for.

Go to your spouse and prepare to do two things. First, apologize for taking him or her for granted – for acting like you were "all that" and like he or she was not significant or needed. Then, let your partner know that you've been doing some thinking and assessing, and you just wanted to take a moment to express your appreciation. In your own way, express yourself to your partner. We won't provide any tips for this part – we think you've got it from here!

@∞

TAKING THE PRINCIPLE TO THE WORKPLACE...

When we do encounter people who act like they are "all that," we are usually more apt to point them out in the workplace. They often do not have a very positive reputation around the office because they come across as if they could dispose of all of the other employees and handle all of the work better all by themselves. These people who shut others and their input down in meetings because to them, their opinion is always the best option. Sometimes, it even seems that they are trying to sabotage you or expose just how inadequate you really are in order to shine the light on their greatness.

If you've never had workplace encounters like this, congratulations! We hope that you make it through your career without them. On the other hand, if you have had workplace encounters like this, you're definitely not alone. If you *are* this person, we can help you do something essential to your career: we can help you see the advantage of identifying and utilizing the strengths of others for your benefit. How do you know if you are this person? If you have heard at any time while you were in school or while you were on the job that you were a know-it-all, bossy, arrogant, proud, cut-throat, or not a team player; this just *might* be you. Whether you accept this or not, just in case, keep reading through the tips. They can't hurt, right? In addition to the preceding tips in the marriage, which will most definitely help you in your interpersonal relationships in the workplace (because the same principles do apply), try embracing the following tips as well.

◉◉

Tip 1: Understand the Truth about Differences

This concept is so important that we'll start this tip out with the bottom line: different does not mean "wrong", different simply means "different." When people look, act, or think differently from us, we are often quick to brand them and their ways as "wrong." When their recommendations and ideas are different from ours, they are instantly "wrong", and we might even become threatened by them. Different simply means different. Even when people are vastly different from you, they still have so much to offer you, but only if you are willing to value their different perspectives and contributions!

No two people are just alike, which means that no two people will think alike or act alike 100% of the time. This means you cannot expect people to think or act like you 100% of the time either– even people who are very similar to you. When they do not, there really is nothing wrong with them, they're only different. The reality is if you give five different people the exact same project to complete within the exact same timeframe, they may take five different approaches to accomplish the same goal, and they'll all get it done in a timely, quality manner. They take different approaches because they are different people, but that does not mean they all can't win in the end!

So that you don't forget, let us remind you that you, alone, are not "all that"! Do not always assume that your way is the right way for everyone else, no matter how well it's worked for you in life. Other people's ways have worked for them as well, and guess what

– their way is often different from your way. Remember: we can do more, together, than we can apart!

❦

Tip 2: Actively Seek Out the Strengths in Others

When you learn to find strengths in people who are different from you (versus only in people who are similar to you), you open yourself up to a rich new pool of resources that you can tap into for the workplace. The challenge, here, is that when people are different from you, their strengths will not be as obvious or glaring to you – because remember, their strengths are of a different type than yours and, thus, not readily identifiable. Consequently, you will have to actively search out the strengths in people who are different from you. If you seek them, you will find them!

When you're actively searching out strengths in the workplace (and yes, *everyone* has them), realize that just about every trait someone has can be used as a strength to help accomplish a goal. For example, playful people may seem unfocused, but when others need to be motivated, he's your guy! The pleasant, passive person who is quiet and, seemingly, not-so-dynamic yet are always at work on time and reliable has a strength of stabilizing the environment and keeping things going. The serious, intense person that prefers to work alone with his computer and moves slowly has the strength of being very research-oriented, calculating, and excellent at generating statistics. The less-personable, aggressive and demanding person, though blatant and forceful, has the strength of being an excellent project leader when you need someone to manage a project through to completion. Regardless of how different your co-workers are from you, their personalities and skills can be used as strengths, if clearly identified and properly directed!

❦

Tip 3: Embrace the Value of Teamwork

Two heads are better than one. If you've not learned this yet in life, as the older folks say, "keep living." When thinking through a process or completing a project, your perspectives has certain limits. When you bring another person into the equation, you now have access to his or her education, experiences and intellect, and so goes it with each additional person and so on. Now access to these additional resources should seem like a great opportunity to you, unless you, honestly, believe that you have the absolute best answer and are not willing to entertain the idea that these other people can have anything of value to offer. In other words, it's a great opportunity unless you believe you're "all that".

You can always go further in life working with a team than you can by yourself. If you are an individualist, this concept may seem wrong to you, but believe it! Surely you've heard the stories of the superstar basketball players who scored unbelievable points and yet their teams suffered loss after loss. That's because there were other players on the team with strengths that went untapped. It wasn't until the superstar gave up some of the glory and some of the point statistics and started working with his team that they all began to win.

This concept is as true in the workplace as on the basketball court. You can try to do everything yourself, but what good is this if your team is not winning? Your being a team player is a lot more attractive to an employer than your being an individualist. While you might be able to complete two projects a month by yourself, if you join together to use the strengths and resources of your team, you could complete five projects a month, possibly resulting in raises or promotions for everyone. This only matters, though, if you are concerned about the success of those other than yourself. If you stop focusing on your strengths long enough, you will learn that other people really do have something valuable to contribute. Here's your final reminder: you're not "all that" by yourself!

Principle 9 Power Points...

- You are a unique, one-of-a-kind original, and everyone else is different from you. However, different does not mean "wrong." Different simply means "different."

- Whether in the marriage or the workplace, don't just learn to tolerate the differences of others, learn to respect, appreciate, and welcome them!

- We can do more together than we can apart – Teamwork!

Principle 10: Politeness & Courtesy Never Go Out of Style

Remember to Say "Please" and "Thank You"

UNDERSTANDING THE PRINCIPLE...

We saved this short, sweet principle for last, because though it is a simple one, it is one that we want to make sure you remember! Common courtesy in our society today is rapidly becoming not-so-common. Whereas words like "please" and "thank you" used to be standard fixtures in our vocabularies, for many, they have become a thing of the past, along with a general sense of politeness, courtesy, and gratitude.

What causes people to cast off important virtues like these? While there are various reasons, perhaps the most prevalent is a sense of entitlement. Entitlement means that instead of feeling a sense of gratitude for something, a person feels like they are owed what they are given, and as a result, they feel no need to say "please" or "thank you." They lack appreciation, because they do feel that what was done for them *should* have been done, thus no appreciation is necessary. In return for what they have received, they feel they owe you nothing, including a "thank you." It doesn't take a genius to figure out that they cannot reasonably expect to receive such kindness and generosity in the future.

In every arena of life, appreciation goes a long way in helping you to get to your destination. When you express appreciation for something, it is a clear sign that you value *both* what was done for you and the individual who did it for you. In turn, the giver is more inclined to repeat the action, and you are more likely to be the beneficiary of their generosity once again. This is key to remember when you desire for a behavior towards you to be repeated in the future. If you want someone to do it again, show your appreciation. It's easy, and it's free!

What does using the term "please" say about us? Well, the term in and of itself is an indication that the person who is requesting something does not take for granted that it would be given if simply requested. Thus, he or she adds on a "please." Or perhaps it's because it sounds extra polite to say "please" that people tag it onto their requests. Even this carries weight, because it is an indication that the requestor is taking intentional efforts to be polite with the request rather than making a demand.

What can be assumed when people do not say "please"? Not saying "please" is directly tied to not saying "thank you" because they both go back to having a sense of entitlement. Essentially, it is indicative of their belief that they do not need to go the extra mile to move you to give them what they desire because you should be doing it for them in the first place. Thus, their request sounds like a demand. As expected, people who make demands in this fashion cannot expect to achieve very good results. None of us responds very well to demands.

❦

TAKING THE PRINCIPLE TO THE
MARRIAGE/RELATIONSHIP...

When we first meet one another and enter a relationship, we tend to be polite and 'on our toes' – especially when we're dating. The man opens the door for the woman, and she says "thank you." The guy takes the girl out to dinner and picks up the check, and she says, "thank you." The young woman wipes the sweat off the forehead of the young man and he says, "thank you." Everything is "please" and "thank you." The longer we stay together in relationships, the more comfortable – and the less courteous and polite - we become with one another.

At the beginning of the relationship, we are intentional about using our courtesy as a tool to help us get what we want; we know that if we are not polite, we will not close the deal on the relationship. However, after we get the phone call for the second date and the relationship goes on for a while, we are less likely to be intentional about these behaviors. This is not to say that we no longer say "please" and "thank you," but we are less intentional about our common courtesies with each other. After all, we have achieved the goal, accomplished the task, and there's nothing else to work for, right?

Time has a way of making us take each other for granted. While we know that we have to be especially courteous to strangers because we have to protect our image. However, when it comes to our partners, well... they're not going anywhere, so we don't feel we have to work so hard to protect our image. Once we get comfortable, we forget to perform those little courtesies that made our spouse love us in the first place. Rather, we believe that if we do our part, they should do their part, and it shouldn't take all of the pleasantries and courtesies for them to do what they are supposed to do because we do our part without need of all of that, right? Thus begins a cycle of mutual disregard when it comes to courtesies. If you walk into many of our households of the people we coach, you will find that most really aren't so polite. They're... well... comfortable and familiar, and these two characteristics tend to erase the necessity of the formality of courtesy. This is unfortunate because partners in the marriage really can use politeness and courtesy to their advantage.

If you recall, we spoke about how if you want someone to repeat a behavior toward you, you should simply express your appreciation. How many times do we nag and criticize our spouse for not doing something around the home? Have you ever considered just going wild with appreciation the next time your spouse does something that you'd like to see repeated? Try this out and see how it works. We assure you that it works a lot better than nagging, criticizing and complaining!

This final principle is simply a reminder to never take your spouse for granted. Once you get to the point of assuming your spouse is going to be there regardless of what you do or don't do, and once you begin assuming that if you no longer open the car door for your sweetheart or say "thank you" when they serve you dinner or take out the trash, it will be hard to redevelop that sense of courtesy. Hold on tight to your courteous habits with your spouse, and never let them go.

❦

TAKING THE PRINCIPLE TO THE WORKPLACE...

The workplace is the social domain where if you are not polite and courteous according to society's standards, people will think you are a jerk! In fact, if you have an inability to pay attention to your use of "please" and "thank you," your co-workers or boss will think you are outright dysfunctional. For the sake of protecting your workplace image, (saying please and thank you), you can expect both resistance and resentment, two of the last things you need while navigating the challenges of the workplace.

The bottom line of this principle in the workplace: you cannot afford to build an unappreciative, demanding type of reputation in the workplace, because once you do, it will be hard to reverse! If you are not already accustomed to being courteous and polite, start now!

Being polite in the workplace will also help you to build allies. When you are not courteous, you repel people instead of them being attracted to you. Further, as we discussed before, once they do something for you and you do not respond courteously to signal your appreciation, they are less likely to ever do anything for you again.

Principle 10 Power Points…

- If you want people to respond favorably and continue sharing generously with you, all it usually takes is a demonstration of appreciation by saying "thank you".

- No one likes being told what to do, and the difference between being told what to do and making a request is the addition of a simple, courteous "please" attached to the end of your request!

ERIC AND ELAINE ON LIFE

"Make Love Work" Relationship Coaching

Request for Speaking Engagement
We appreciate your invitation for us to share our message with your organization! As you can imagine, the Johnson's live a very busy lifestyle and must be selective about the engagements that we choose to accept.

So that we may give your invitation full consideration, please complete the following information and fax or e-mail it back to us. Please allow up to 10 days for a reply once this form has been submitted. Thank you!
- Eric & Elaine Johnson

Organization Name: _____
Address:_____
City: _____ State: _____ Zip: _____

Contact Name:_____ Title:_____
Contact's Office Phone: _____ Mobile Phone:_____
Contact's E-mail Address: _____
Organization's Website Address: _____

Requested Day(s)/Date(s) for Speaking (please include at least two options):
1st Date Option: _____   2nd Date Option: _____
Presentation Time(s): _____   Requested Length of Presentation:_____

Type of Meeting:
( )   Conference   ( ) Workshop/Seminar ( )   Convention
( )   Church Service ( ) Anniversary   ( )   Other _____

Theme of Meeting/Event:_____
Any Special Topic Requested?   (   ) Yes   (   ) No

If Yes, Please List: _____

Location of Meeting (*if different from organization's address*): _____

Physical Address:_____

Telephone: _____

Expected Attendance: _____

Audience Composition (married couples, newlyweds, civic group, general community, etc.):

_____

How Do You Plan to Promote the Event? _____

Other Speakers Participating (*please list their speaking dates and times, and please note whether they are invited or confirmed*):

_____

_____

Form Completed By: _____

Please fax or mail completed form to:

Eric and Elaine On Life
P O Box 300752
Houston, TX 77230-0752

PHONE: 1.800.387.2073
FAX: (832) 460-3747

Product Type	Unit Price	Quantity	Product Subtotal	Shipping Cost*	Total Order Cost
Autographed & Dedicated Copy	$24.99				
Standard Copy	$17.99				

Standard Shipping Rates   *1 – 4 books: $4.95*   *5 – 10 books: $8.95*
11 - 20 books: 12.95

PAYMENT INFO
Form of Payment:

☐   Check   Please make checks payable to: **E Squared Publishing**

☐   Credit Card   _____ Visa   _____ MasterCard
                         _____ Discover _____ AMEX

Charge Amount Authorized: $_____ (please include
                                      shipping cost, if applicable)
Name on Card: _____

Billing Address for Card: _____
_____

City: _____
State: _____ Zip: _____
Credit Card Number: _____Expiration Date: _____ / _____ /

3-digit security code: _____ (Located on the back of the
                                      card after the cc number)
Authorization Signature: _____
Date: _____ / _____ / 20_____

SHIPPING INFO

Note: Please complete only if shipping address is <u>different from</u> billing address.

Name: _____

Phone: _____

Shipping Address: _____

City, State: _____Zip: _____

E-mail: _____

www.ingramcontent.com/pod-product-compliance
Lightning Source LLC
Chambersburg PA
CBHW022113280326
41933CB00007B/371